THE ANFIELD ENCYCLOPEDIA

ACKNOWLEDGMENTS

A particular word of thanks should be given to Steve Hale who has supplied most of the photographs in this book. Thanks should also be given to all those at Mainstream Publishing who have been involved with this project, including Bill Campbell, Peter Frances and Janene Reid, and especially to Stephen Raw for the design of the jacket. I am also grateful to Jim Gardiner and the Association of Football Statisticians for their helpful advice. Thanks are due also to my agent John Pawsey and my gratitude, as ever, to my wife Judith and children Nicholas and Emma.

An A-Z of Liverpool FC

Stephen F. Kelly

MAINSTREAM
PUBLISHING

EDINBURGH AND LONDON

For Judith, Nicholas and Emma

Copyright © Stephen F. Kelly, 1993

First published in Great Britain in 1993 by
MAINSTREAM PUBLISHING COMPANY (EDINBURGH) LTD
7 Albany Street
Edinburgh EH1 3UG

Reprinted 1994

Second edition 1995

ISBN 1 85158 818 3

A catalogue record for this book is available from the British Library

Typeset in 11/13 Janson by Servis Filmsetting Ltd, Manchester

Printed in Great Britain by The Cromwell Press, Melksham, Wiltshire

ABANDONED. Two Liverpool games have had to be abandoned because of crowd problems. The first, against Sheffield United in the 1899 FA Cup semi-final, had to be stopped as the crowd kept spilling on to the pitch. The game was played at Fallowfield in Manchester, venue of the 1893 Cup final. The ground was far too small for the 30,000 crowd who turned up and at half-time the referee, fearing for the safety of the players as well as spectators, called the match off. It was eventually replayed at Derby. Coincidentally, the other game that was called off was also an FA Cup semi-final, at Hillsborough in 1989, when 96 Liverpool supporters were tragically killed in the Leppings Lane end of the ground.

A'COURT, ALAN. Liverpool-born winger who went on to win England honours. Born in 1934, A'Court joined Liverpool on his 18th birthday, making his debut in 1953. He soon established himself on Liverpool's wing, appearing 16 times the following season as Liverpool were relegated, and then became a regular. Yet despite the presence of two outstanding wingers in A'Court and Liddell, Liverpool continued to find it difficult to escape the second division.

He was capped by England in 1957, making his debut against Northern Ireland, and the following year made four further appearances, three of those in the 1958 World Cup finals in Sweden. A small, speedy winger, A'Court was a vital cog in the Liverpool team that finally won promotion in 1962. With the emergence of Peter Thompson, however, A'Court found himself squeezed out of the side and he played his final game for Liverpool against Reykjavik in the second leg of a European Cup tie in September 1964. The following month he moved to Tranmere Rovers where he made more than 50 appearances. At the age of 32 he left Prenton Park and then held various coaching jobs at Norwich, Chester, Crewe and Stoke as well as in Zambia. A'Court also played for the Football League and made seven appearances for the England Under-23s. During his years at Anfield he made a total of 382 appearances, scoring 63 goals.

ABLETT, GARY. Joined Liverpool as an apprentice in 1983, making his Liverpool debut during the 1986–87 season. A tall, useful defender, Ablett could fit in almost anywhere in the back four. He had loan spells with Derby County where he actually made his league debut and then with Hull City. He appeared in the 1989 FA Cup final against Everton and was a regular as Liverpool won the league title in 1988. Capped at England Under-21 level, Ablett was transferred to Everton in 1991 for £750,000 – a signing which surprised Everton supporters more than it did Liverpool fans. He had not always been the most popular player with the fans even though manager Kenny Dalglish had demonstrated his confidence in the young man. Ablett played 109 games for Liverpool.

AGGREGATE SCORE. Liverpool's highest aggregate score in any competition came in the Fairs Cup in September 1969 against Dundalk, when they notched up 14 goals over two legs. Liverpool won the first leg 10–0 at Anfield and then 4–0 in Ireland.

ALDRIDGE, JOHN. Bought by Kenny Dalglish as a replacement for Ian Rush who was set to join Juventus. Liverpool-born Aldridge had supported the club from the Kop in his youth, and, although Liverpool had been interested in him at that stage, he was allowed to join Newport County. In March 1984 Oxford United paid Newport £78,000 for him. It was money well spent, especially as his goals helped them into the first division – and even more so as Liverpool paid more than ten times that amount in January 1987 to bring him back home. Over the next few years he was to prove almost as prolific a goalscorer as Rush. Eventually the return of Rush was to limit his appearances and, in September 1989, he was inevitably transferred, joining the Spanish club Real Socie-dad where he continued to clock up the goals in spite of the notoriously tight marking of Spanish defences. He joined Tranmere Rovers during the summer of 1991 and netted a record 40 goals for them in his first season. Although he had been born in Liverpool, Aldridge opted to play for the Republic of Ireland and has been capped more than 50 times. But, surprisingly, goals at an international level seem to have been far harder to come by than in club games: he

John Aldridge

has only a handful to his credit. A ferocious and accurate penalty-taker, Aldridge missed only once for Liverpool, in the FA Cup final against Wimbledon. It was to be the most important miss of his life, robbing Liverpool of a much-deserved double. He played a total of 83 league matches for the Reds scoring a remarkable 50 goals, and was a great favourite with the Kop. Even though he spent only a few years at Anfield, Aldridge's heart has, without doubt, always belonged to the club.

ALLAN, GEORGE. The Scottish centre-forward joined Liverpool from Leith Athletic in 1895. He initially spent two years at Anfield and then departed for Celtic, only to return a year later. During his three years with Liverpool Allan played 97 games and scored a spectacular 60 goals, making him one of the most prolific goalscorers in the club's history. A strong, agile centre-forward, Allan was the spearhead of Liverpool's attack as they clinched the second division championship in 1896, scoring 25 goals in just 20 appearances, as Liverpool rattled in 106 goals in 30 league games. The following season he scored 17 league goals before joining Celtic where he won a Scottish league championship medal. But a year later he was back at Anfield, playing a full season, though netting only eight goals in 30 games, as Liverpool finished the season runners-up and FA Cup semi-finalists. The reason for his poor scoring form soon became apparent; Allan had contracted tuberculosis and in October that year died tragically at the early age of 24. Allan was Liverpool's first ever Scottish international but was capped just once, scoring twice in the 3–2 defeat of England at Ewood Park in 1897.

AMATEURS. Although Liverpool boasted many amateurs in the early days, only a few have played for the club since the Second World War. They include Doug Rudham, the South African goalkeeper, Len Charney, Alan Arnell, Albert Childs, Peter Kippax and Barry Wilkinson. Perhaps the most famous of recent years was Steve Heighway who made his Liverpool debut in 1970 and turned professional almost immediately.

ANDERSON, ERIC. Inside-forward who played with the club during the 1950s. Came to Anfield from the Army in 1951, making 73 league appearances over the next six years. He was transferred to Barnsley in July 1957 for £4,000 and later played with Bournemouth.

ANFIELD. Originally the home of Everton Football Club. The first game ever played at Anfield was on 28 September 1884 when Everton beat Earlstown 5–0. Anfield hosted its first league game four years later on 8 September 1888 when the visitors, Accrington Stanley, were beaten 2–1. But in 1892 a row over the tenancy and rent led to the members of the Everton Football Club storming out to find new premises. John Houlding, the official tenant of the ground, found an easy solution – he formed a new club and, of course, named it Liverpool. Today you would be hard put to find anything that remains of the old Anfield ground. New stands and a new Kop have entirely transformed the ground, making it one of Britain's super stadiums. The capacity by 1995 had been reduced from its record high of 61,905 to around 42,000.

Liverpool's first game at Anfield was a friendly played on the evening of Thursday, 1 September 1892, against Rotherham. Liverpool won 7–1. In the early days attendances were never much more than 5,000 but as the club's reputation began to grow, so they constructed new facilities to cope with higher attendances. A new stand with a red and white central gable was built in 1895 on the site of the current Main Stand and another stand was also built at the Anfield Road End in 1903, constructed out of timber and corrugated iron. Then in 1906, after Liverpool had won the league championship, a huge banking was built behind the goal at the Walton Breck Road End of the ground. It was christened the Kop and soon became one of the most famous terracings in football. Around the same time a stand was also built on the Kemlyn Road. The stadium remained much the same until 1928 when the Kop was extended and roofed. In 1957 floodlights were installed and then six years later the Kemlyn Road Stand was replaced with a new cantilever stand costing £350,000. A few years later alterations were made at the Anfield Road End, turning it into a large covered standing area. After that came the new Main Stand, built in 1973, and then during the summer of 1992 a second tier was added to the Kemlyn Road stand as well as executive boxes and dining suites. During the summer of 1994 the Kop was demolished with a new stand built providing seats for 13,000 spectators.

ANFIELD ROAD END. Known to most fans as the 'Annie Road End', this is the section behind the goal at the Anfield Road end of the ground. Over the years it has undergone many changes. At one time there was a stand, built in 1903,

The new Centenary Stand at Anfield

which was eventually torn down to be replaced by terracing and a roof. In recent years the terracing has given way to seating, with a large proportion allocated to visiting fans. By 1993 there were 3,120 seats for visitors and 2,392 seats for home supporters.

APPEARANCES. Ian Callaghan holds the record for the number of appearances in a Liverpool shirt, with a total of 843 games to his credit between 1960 and 1978. In all, Callaghan played 637 league games, 42 Football League Cup games, 77 FA Cup games and 87 European matches. He also made a number of appearances as a substitute.

ARNELL, ALAN. You either loved him or you hated him, but in 69 league appearances Alan Arnell did manage an impressive 33 goals. He signed for the club as an amateur in 1953, making his debut that same year, and turned professional in 1954. He even scored on his debut as Liverpool slammed five goals past Blackpool, but it was not enough to save Liverpool from relegation and by the end of the season the club ended up at the bottom of the league. The rest of Arnell's Anfield days were then spent in second division football. In February 1961, just as Liverpool were beginning to drag themselves out of the division, Arnell was sold to Tranmere in Shankly's big Anfield clear-out.

ARROWSMITH, ALF. Manchester-born Arrowsmith played a useful role in Liverpool's championship winning team of 1963–64. An inside-forward, he joined Liverpool from Ashton United in August 1960 and, over the next eight years, made 50 appearances, scoring a creditable 24 goals. In the championship season he took over from Jimmy Melia and managed 15 league goals in just 20 matches. After that his appearances were surprisingly few and far between, and in December 1968 he was transferred to Bury for £25,000.

ASHCROFT, CHARLIE. Goalkeeper with 87 league appearances to his credit but who never really became a regular. He had joined Liverpool during the war but had to wait until September 1946 before making his league debut – the same day as Bob Paisley – when Liverpool thrashed Chelsea 7–4 at Anfield. Unfortunately he made only one other appearance that season, with Cyril Sidlow remaining first choice for the goalkeeper's jersey. In 1955 he left to join Ipswich.

ASHWORTH, DAVID. Manager of Liverpool for just three years during the early 1920s. In his first season in charge Liverpool wound up in fourth spot but the following year they clinched their third league title with one of the finest of all Anfield sides that included players such as Elisha Scott, Dick Forshaw, Don McKinlay, Harry Chambers, Tom Bromilow and Tom Lucas. A year later Liverpool again captured the title but before the end of the season Ashworth had gone, joining bottom-of-the-table Oldham Athletic for reasons that have always remained something of a mystery. Oldham, however, were relegated while Liverpool went on to lift their fourth title. It was Ashworth's second spell at Oldham: he had originally taken them from the Lancashire Combination to the first division. He later managed Manchester City and Walsall. A small man – he was said to be no more than five feet tall – he usually sported a well-greased moustache and a bowler hat. He was also a former referee. He died in 1947, aged 79.

ATTENDANCE – HIGHEST. The record attendance at Anfield is 61,905 for the fourth round FA Cup game with Wolverhampton Wanderers on 2 February 1952. Liverpool won 2–1 with goals from Bob Paisley and Cyril Done. The record attendance for a league match was on 27 December 1949 when 58,757 watched Liverpool and Chelsea fight out a 2–2 draw.

B

BABB, PHIL. Defender signed by Liverpool early in the 1994/95 season after giving some impressive displays for Ireland in the World Cup finals. Babb arrived at Anfield from Coventry City for £3.5 million, making him one of the most expensive defenders in Britain. He began his Anfield career playing out of position and took time to adapt but by the end of his first season had picked up a winners' medal in the Coca-Cola Cup and even more international honours. Babb was born in Lambeth and began his footballing career with Millwall but left the London club before he had made any appearances for them. He then joined Bradford City where he made more than 80 appearances but left them to join Coventry.

BALMER, JACK. The nephew of the famous Everton full-backs William and Robert Balmer. Not surprisingly he joined Everton as an amateur, but failed to make the grade and in May 1935 crossed Stanley Park to join Liverpool, also as an amateur. Born in Liverpool, Jack Balmer played almost 300 league games for the Reds, scoring 99 goals. He picked up a league championship medal in 1947. A goalscoring inside-forward, he made his league debut in

September 1935. During the war he guested for Brighton and Newcastle but later returned to Anfield to help Liverpool clinch their fifth league title. Balmer scored 24 league goals that season and also had the distinction of hitting three consecutive hat tricks – three goals at home against Portsmouth, four away at Derby and three against Arsenal at home – to become the first player ever to achieve this feat. His three hat tricks began a goalscoring sequence in which he scored 15 goals in seven consecutive matches. Although Balmer skippered the Liverpool side, he was not the most popular player with the fans who thought him stand-offish. Nor was he ever capped by England, although he was a trialist and did play in some unofficial wartime internationals.

BAMBER, JACK. Born in St Helens, Jack Bamber came to Anfield just after the First World War had begun but did not make his league debut until 1919. Over the next nine years he was to prove an effective half-back, going on to win an England cap in 1921 to add to the two representative games he had played on the FA tour of South Africa in 1920. He would undoubtedly have won many more honours but unfortunately injury struck and he was an absentee for a couple of seasons as Liverpool clinched two successive championships. He was never capped again by England and in 1924 after 80 appearances, mainly at right-half, he signed for Leicester City, helping them to the second division championship. He later played with Tranmere Rovers.

BARCLAY, W. E. The first Liverpool manager who, between 1892 and 1896, served alongside the club's guiding spirit, John McKenna. At the turn of the century the role of secretary and manager were usually the same and it was no different at Anfield. McKenna served in both capacities although he was ably helped with matters on the field by Barclay. Both men had been involved with Everton Football Club when they were at Anfield but remained loyal to John

Houlding when the split saw Everton move to Goodison Park. Barclay is credited with much of the good work that led to Liverpool's early successes, although he was apparently opposed to the club joining the Football League. But once they had joined, Barclay dashed off on many a trip north to sign new players and laid a secure foundation for the club's future.

BARGAIN BUYS. Over the years Liverpool have made many bargain buys, usually from the lower divisions. It was a policy developed and encouraged by Bill Shankly. Kevin Keegan must rank as one of the all-time bargains, having been bought for a mere £33,000 from Scunthorpe. He was later sold to Hamburg for £500,000. Ray Clemence was another bargain from Scunthorpe – costing around £15,000 – who went on to play 61 games for England. Another man who had a long and illustrious England career was Phil Neal, bought for £65,000 from Northampton. From Scotland came Alan Hansen, costing £100,000 from Partick Thistle. Many, however, would argue that Kenny Dalglish, although he cost a British record fee of £440,000, turned out to be the bargain of all time. In more recent years, the £300,000 signing of Rob Jones from Crewe looks like another bargain buy.

BARNES, JOHN. The signing of John Barnes during the summer of 1987 was greeted with some scepticism by many Liverpool supporters. For weeks the 'will he or won't he sign' headlines had been dominating the back pages, with Barnes said to be holding out for a better offer from a top continental club. There was also a school of thought that Barnes was perhaps a little too individualistic for the Liverpool style. But eventually the Watford winger signed for a fee of £900,000 and almost from the start set the Football League and Merseyside alight with his exhilarating displays. Dalglish's intuition had paid off yet again. With Peter Beardsley also added to the attack as well as Ray Houghton in the midfield, Liverpool took on a new look.

John Barnes

The endeavour and commitment that had been the hallmark of so many Liverpool sides of the past suddenly gave way to a new adventurous flair, epitomised by Barnes' dashing chases down the flanks. He was a revelation. Fêted so often at Watford, Barnes had never really shown the same spirit in an England shirt – although one of his mazy dances through the Brazilian defence had resulted in what was described as the best goal ever scored in the Maracana stadium. Suddenly Barnes was repeating it at Anfield and the crowds flocked to see him with the 'gates closed' signs going up every week. When he was on the ball there was a sense of expectation. Against Queens Park Rangers he pulled the ball over the halfway line and began a run that swept him past four defenders before he fired a low shot into the corner of the net. By the time he was approaching the penalty area the whole of Anfield was on its feet. That season Liverpool went an astonishing 29 league games from the start of the season before they were eventually beaten, and by the end of the campaign Barnes had been voted

Player of the Year by both the Football Writers and the PFA.

Born in Jamaica in 1963, the son of a top-ranking army officer and a leading television presenter, Barnes came to England for his education. He was soon spotted by Watford and signed for them in July 1981. Under the guidance of Watford manager Graham Taylor, Barnes' career began to develop and he was a member of the Watford Cup final side beaten by Everton in 1984. Already a seasoned England international by the time of his move to Anfield, Barnes has now been capped more than 70 times by his country. Yet he somehow still continues to disappoint at an international level, never seemingly capable of reproducing his club form on the world stage. But at Liverpool his displays have continued to electrify spectators. He won first division championship honours in 1988 and 1990 and a Cup winners' medal in 1989 but missed much of the 1991–92 season through injury, returning to the side only in late 1992. During the 1994–95 season Barnes took up a new position operating immediately in front of the defence. With his ability to hold the ball and set up passes it was to prove highly effective and was a major factor in Liverpool's Coca-Cola Cup victory.

BARON, KEVIN. Post-war inside-forward fondly remembered by Kopites for his intricate ball skills. His record of 33 goals in 152 appearances also speaks volumes, although at the end of his days he had little to show in the way of honours. He was not a member of the post-war championship side although he did play in Liverpool's losing FA Cup final team in 1950. Born in Preston, he joined Liverpool in 1944 and remained with the club for ten years before moving to Southend. He later played with Northampton and Aldershot as well as a host of non-league clubs.

BEARDSLEY, PETER. When Peter Beardsley joined Liverpool from Newcastle United for £1.8 million during the summer of 1987, it was the most expensive transfer deal

Peter Beardsley

between British clubs. For many years Beardsley had been something of an enigma. His career had begun with Carlisle United where he showed considerable potential, but no first division club seemed prepared to pay Carlisle's asking price. Eventually the Canadian club Vancouver Whitecaps stepped in with a bid and Beardsley was soon on his way across the Atlantic. Playing against Manchester United in a pre-season friendly some years later, Beardsley impressed United manager Ron Atkinson so much that he paid £250,000 for him. Unfortunately Beardsley failed to make the grade at Old Trafford, appearing as a substitute for just 45 minutes. United let him drift back to Canada but he eventually wound up in his home town of Newcastle where all his talents suddenly began to blossom. He was a revelation and within a couple of years had become the hottest property in British soccer. It seemed inevitable that he would end up at Anfield. Playing alongside John Barnes and John Aldridge, Beardsley looked a class player, and an early season goal against Arsenal at Anfield when he drifted through the Gunners' defence to slam the ball into the back of the net will long be remembered by Kopites. Beardsley was an outstanding player during that season but somehow seemed to run out of steam in later seasons, at times appearing reluctant to take the ball forward. His confidence was not helped when Dalglish left him out of the side on a number of occasions for tactical reasons. At the time he was the league's leading goalscorer and it was difficult to comprehend the manager's game plan. Perhaps in the end Beardsley never quite had the ability or determination to become a world-class player. He seemed to lack the biting edge, and when Graeme Souness took over from Dalglish the manager had no qualms in selling him to Everton for £1 million. It was a move which raised a few eyebrows around Anfield, but with Dean Saunders just signed it seemed that Liverpool had a proliferation of forwards. In the event injuries and the disappointing form of Saunders meant that Beardsley's absence was missed far more than anyone had anticipated. Yet despite the problems Beardsley's days at Anfield were littered with honours. He won two championship medals, an FA Cup winners' medal and further England caps to add to his growing collection. During the summer of 1993 Everton sold him to his former club Newcastle United for £1.5m.

BECTON, FRANK. Born in Preston in 1873, Frank Becton began his footballing days with Preston North End and was transferred to Liverpool for the princely sum of £100 in March 1895. An inside-forward, he helped Liverpool towards the second division championship in 1896, scoring 17 goals in 24 appearances. He made a total of 74 appearances for Liverpool, scoring 37 times, before he was transferred to Sheffield United in 1898. He later played for Preston North End again, Swindon and New Brighton Tower, before ill health caught up with him. He died of tuberculosis in 1909. He was capped once by England while at Liverpool, in a match where England beat Wales 4–0. His only other cap came in 1895 when he was a Preston player: England beat Ireland 9–0 with the 21-year-old Becton scoring twice. He also represented the Football League twice.

BEGLIN, JIM. Tall, slim Irish defender who joined Liverpool from Shamrock Rovers in May 1983. Beglin made his league debut a year later and looked set for a long Liverpool career until he broke a leg against Everton in 1987. It was a particularly serious injury which sidelined him for almost a year. When he did return, he suffered a second nasty leg injury in a reserve outing. He made a brief recovery but was unable to regain his place and was transferred to Leeds United. Unfortunately the injury continued to dog him and eventually Beglin was forced to quit the game prematurely, bringing a sad end to what might have been a glittering career. Beglin won first division championship honours with Liverpool as well as an FA Cup winners' medal. He also appeared for Liverpool in the ill-fated European Cup final against Juventus at the Heysel stadium.

BENNETT, REUBEN. Liverpool trainer who served under Bill Shankly for many years and was one of the first ever members of the famous Liverpool boot room.

BERRY, ARTHUR. Has the distinction of being not only a graduate of Oxford University and the holder of two Oxford Blues but was also the winner of two Olympic gold medals. Berry was born in Liverpool in 1888, the son of one of the club's directors who served as chairman between 1904 and 1909. Berry was a leading amateur footballer, winning his Oxford Blues in 1908 and 1909. In 1907 he had joined Liverpool but two years later went off to play for Fulham. He also had a short spell with Everton during the 1909–10 season but returned to Liverpool in 1912 for a season. He played 32 times for the Great Britain amateur side, winning his gold medals in the 1908 and the 1912 Olympics. Berry later became a barrister. He made just four appearances for the Reds, all as a forward.

BIMPSON, LOUIS. Liverpool centre-forward of the 1950s who played most of his games in the second division. He made his league debut in March 1953 and went on to play 100 games, scoring 40 goals – a highly respectable tally. Yet Bimpson never quite looked the part. His best seasons were 1953–54 when Liverpool were relegated as he notched up 13 goals in 24 appearances, and 1958–59 when he struck 11 goals in 15 appearances. Transferred to Blackburn Rovers in 1959, he played in their losing FA Cup final side a year later.

BJORNEBYE, STIG. Norwegian defender signed from the Norwegian club Rosenberg in late 1992. Liverpool had played Rosenberg during their pre-season tour of Norway and had been impressed by the 22-year-old. Bjornebye cost Liverpool £600,000 but, as an experienced international, he was soon being rated as a bargain buy. He stepped into the first team immediately but lost his place towards the end of the 1992-93 season. After the dismissal of Graeme Souness, Bjornebye returned to the side, doubling as a midfielder and defender. He was a regular for most of the season and a member of Liverpool's Coca-Cola Cup winning side but was unfortunately sidelined towards the end of the season after breaking his leg at Anfield.

BLENKINSOP, ERNIE. During the pre-war years Liverpool boasted a pair of England full-backs in their defence. One of those was Ernie Blenkinsop, an expensive purchase when Liverpool signed him from Sheffield Wednesday for £5,000 in March 1934. Unfortunately Blenkinsop, by then in his mid-30s, was at the tail end of his career. All his caps had been won with Sheffield Wednesday – an impressive 26 – and a not inconsiderable number for those days, especially as they had been won consecutively, then a record for England. He captained England on his final appearance and played for the Football League. He went on to play 74 games for Liverpool as a left-back, partnering Tom Cooper. After three years at Anfield he joined Cardiff City.

BOERSMA, PHIL. In a long career at Anfield Boersma never quite established himself. A Liverpool lad, he joined the club during the mid-1960s, making his league debut in September 1969. With Toshack injured during the 1972–73 season Boersma was given an extended run and picked up a league championship medal. The following season he found himself sidelined but began the 1973–74 season in blistering form, hitting six goals in the first eight league games. Unfortunately his goalscoring then dried up and he did not hit target again throughout the entire season – Boersma was that kind of a player. In second division soccer he might have done extremely well, but in the top flight chances did not fall easily, and when they did they had to be snapped up. In December 1975 he was transferred to Middlesbrough and later had spells with Swansea and Luton. He later wound up as assistant manager to Graeme Souness at Glasgow Rangers and then returned to his old haunts when Souness took over at Anfield but left Anfield when Souness was sacked.

BOOKS. Among the many books that have been written about Liverpool Football Club are:
Brian Pead, *Liverpool: A Complete Record*
Stephen F. Kelly, *You'll Never Walk Alone*
Stephen F. Kelly, *Liverpool in Europe*
Percy M. Young, *Football On Merseyside*
Ivan Ponting and Steve Hale, *The Boot Room*
Phil Thompson, *Shankly*

BOOT ROOM. The Liverpool boot room, famed throughout football, was really the creation of Bill Shankly. It was here that Shankly and his backroom staff would gather after training and matches to mull over problems. It was their den where many a victory was plotted. Over the years its members have included not only Shankly but Bob Paisley, Reuben Bennett, Tom Saunders, Joe Fagan, Kenny Dalglish, Ronnie Moran, Roy Evans, Graeme Souness and Phil Boersma. It was demolished in early 1993.

BOXING. During the 1920s and 1930s boxing was a regular feature at Anfield. A number of British championships were contested there and on 12 June 1934 Nelson Tarleton fought for the world featherweight title against the American holder Freddie Miller. The fight went to a points decision with Miller retaining his title.

BRADLEY, JIM. Left-half of the Edwardian era with 169 league appearances to his name, Bradley joined Liverpool from Stoke City in September 1905 and was a member of the championship-winning side of the following season. He represented the Football League but never managed a full England cap. Bradley joined Reading in 1911 and eventually returned to Stoke in 1913.

BRADSHAW, HARRY. The first Liverpool player to win an England cap, Bradshaw joined Liverpool from Northwich

Bootroom Boys

23

Victoria in October 1893 and scored on his debut. He spent two years at Anfield, during which time he collected two second division championship medals and his only England cap, when he played for England in February 1897 in the 6–0 defeat of Ireland at Nottingham. Bradshaw could play in virtually any forward position and was Liverpool's top scorer in 1895. He left Anfield in 1898 for Tottenham Hotspur, then a Southern League side, and a year after signed for Thames Ironworks, later to become West Ham United. He died suddenly on Christmas Day 1899, aged 26.

BRADSHAW, TOM. Always known as 'Tiny' Bradshaw because of his 6ft 2ins height. Bradshaw was an elegant centre-half with the build and style of an Alan Hansen. Like Hansen, he was Scottish and although he was capped only once by his country it was against England in 1928 when the famous Wembley Wizards ran the English dizzy to win 5–1. Unfortunately Bradshaw was merely standing in that day for the great David Meiklejohn; when the Rangers man returned from injury Bradshaw found himself sidelined and was never capped again. At that stage of his career he was with Bury but joined Liverpool in January 1930 for £8,000, a huge fee for those days. In his later Anfield days he linked up with Matt Busby and Jimmy McDougall to form a famous all-Scottish half-back line. Bradshaw was a superb central defender, powerful and sure, and a match for most attackers, including Dixie Dean, who rated him the best centre-half of all. He left Liverpool in 1938, after almost 300 appearances, and joined Third Lanark.

BRIERLEY, KEN. Began life at Oldham Athletic after the war as an inside-forward, attracting much comment with his skilful displays. He was transferred to Liverpool in February 1948 for what was then a considerable fee. Liverpool immediately converted him into a wing-half and over the next five years he made 59 appearances, scoring nine goals. In 1953 he returned to Oldham for £2,500 and helped them towards the third division north title.

BROMILOW, TOM. England international who played all his football with Liverpool. Liverpool-born Bromilow was invalided out of the army during the First World War, so came to Anfield and asked for a trial. Within two years he was playing for England. He made his league debut in October 1919 and went on playing until 1930, making 374 appearances. Bromilow was a fine left-half, assured and strong, who won the first of his five England caps in 1921. He had earlier played for the North team that thrashed an England XI 6–1. When he retired he took up a coaching position in Amsterdam but returned a year later to embark on a highly successful managerial career, first with Burnley, and then with Crystal Palace and Leicester. He was also the brother-in-law of Theo Kelly, the manager and secretary of Everton.

BURKINSHAW, KEITH. Although Keith Burkinshaw made only one appearance for Liverpool he later went on to become a successful football manager. He joined Liverpool in 1953, making his solitary appearance in April 1955. Two years later he went to Workington and then Scunthorpe. He eventually began a coaching career with Newcastle United in 1968 before joining Tottenham Hotspur as chief coach. In 1976 he became manager of Spurs, a position he held until 1984. He later served as manager of the Bahrain national squad and at Gillingham.

BURROWS, DAVID. Young defender signed from West Bromwich Albion in 1988 for £500,000. Burrows was something of a gamble for manager Dalglish: he was forced to pay out a huge fee for the teenager, who had only played a handful of games for the Midlands club. But Dalglish trusted his instinct and Burrows was thrown into the fray almost immediately. He remained a regular choice at full-back, happy to play on either side of defence. Strong, aggressive and a tough tackler, Burrows was at times criticised for his over-enthusiasm which led to more than a few bookings. He liked to get forward and his overlaps with John Barnes resulted in many a Liverpool goal. Capped at England Under-21 level. In September 1993 Graeme Souness sold him to West Ham United along with Mike Marsh in a deal that brought Julian Dicks to Anfield.

BUSBY, MATT. Joined Liverpool from Manchester City in March 1936 for £8,000. A stylish wing-half, Busby's flagging career was suddenly revived at Anfield where he joined an all-Scottish half-back line, one of the finest in Liverpool's history. Busby had joined Manchester City as a youngster and went on to play more than 200 games for the Maine Road club, appearing in the 1933 and 1934 Cup finals. He played over 100 league games for Liverpool, yet in a long and illustrious career was surprisingly capped only once by his country. During the war he guested for a number of clubs including Chelsea, Middlesbrough and Bournemouth, and played in a number of wartime inter-nationals. After the war Liverpool offered him a position on their coaching staff but while he was considering the prospect Manchester United jumped in and offered him the job of manager at Old Trafford. The rest, as they say, is history. Under Busby United went on to win five league titles and two FA Cups, and became the first English side to lift the European Cup. Seriously injured in the Munich disaster, Busby was not expected to live. Yet within months he was at Wembley watching his makeshift side go down to Bolton Wanderers in the 1958 Cup final. A year earlier his team, fondly known as the 'Busby Babes', had come within a whisker of clinching the Double. Busby will almost certainly go down as one of the greatest managers the English game has ever seen, his principal claim to fame being that he guided three totally different Manchester United sides to the championship.

BUSH, TOM. Like so many fine players of his generation, Tom Bush's best years were interrupted by war service. He came to Liverpool in 1933 and made just 64 league appearances as a half-back before war broke out. During the war he guested with a number of clubs and was still on Liverpool's books when peace returned. But by then he was too old for first division football and he retired in 1947. He coached briefly in Holland before returning to Anfield as a coach.

BYRNE, GERRY. Famed full-back of the 1960s whose finest moment came at Wembley in 1965 as Liverpool lifted the FA Cup for the first time in their history. Injured after just three minutes, Byrne bravely played on into extra time as if nothing had happened. It was revealed after the game that he had in fact broken his collar bone. Born in Liverpool, Byrne joined the Anfield staff in 1955 straight from school and went on to play 273 games for the Reds, winning league championship honours, an FA Cup winners' medal and two England caps. But his early career had looked unpromising. After putting one into his own net on his debut he was largely ignored until the arrival of Bill Shankly turned him into one of the surest defenders in the first division. Injury forced him to retire in 1969, when he joined the coaching staff for a short while. A stylish full-back who could play on either the left or right, Byrne formed an effective partnership with Chris Lawler that was the backbone of an outstanding Liverpool side.

C

CADDEN, JOSEPH. Although he played just four games for the club Joe Cadden deserves an entry simply for the fact that he was the first Liverpool player to be signed from an American club, not long after the Second World War. Cadden was actually born in Glasgow but immediately after he had been demobbed he went to America where he started playing soccer for the Brooklyn Wanderers. When Liverpool toured America during the summer of 1948 they played the Brooklyn Wanderers and were sufficiently impressed by the centre-half to offer him a contract. But it never really worked out. He made just four appearances, the first in September 1950, and two years later he joined Grimsby Town where he made only one appearance before moving on to Accrington Stanley. He later had a spell with New Brighton.

CALLAGHAN, IAN. One of the club's finest and certainly its most loyal servant, playing a record 636 league games and a total of 843 games in a 21-year career at Anfield. Born in Liverpool, Callaghan joined the ground staff in 1957 and made his debut in a second division game against Rotherham in April 1960: he was applauded off the field by his

Ian Callaghan

team-mates. Over the next two decades he would win every honour in the game. He even played in the 1966 World Cup finals and won a total of four England caps. He holds the record gap between caps: having played twice for England in 1966, he was not chosen again until October 1977, a gap of 11 years and 49 days. Callaghan was also awarded the MBE and was the Football Writers' Player of the Year in 1974. On top of all that he won European, league championship and FA Cup winners' medals before he finally quit the club to join Swansea in September 1978.

Only 5ft 7ins, Callaghan began his footballing life as an outside-right but as the vogue for wingers disappeared he was converted into a midfielder, though with the licence to roam down the flanks. He was nippy, a fine crosser of the ball and a thoughtful player who rarely delivered a bad pass. He scored a total of 69 goals for Liverpool, 49 of them in the league. He was an outstanding example to all the young players at Anfield, never losing his temper on the field or deliberately committing a bad foul and was never sent off in his long career.

CAMPBELL, BOBBY. Made just 14 appearances for Liverpool as a wing-half during the club's second division days of the late 1950s and early 1960s. Born in Liverpool, he joined the club in May 1954. He left in 1961 to join Wigan Athletic and later played with a number of clubs including Portsmouth and Aldershot. He became better known, however, as a coach and manager with jobs at QPR, Arsenal, Fulham, Chelsea and Portsmouth.

CAMPBELL, KENNY. One in a long line of outstanding Anfield goalkeepers, Campbell joined Liverpool from the Scottish club Cambuslang Rovers in May 1911. He took over from the great Sam Hardy in 1912 and was the regular choice until the First World War. He played just one season after the war and moved on to Partick Thistle in April 1920 when Elisha Scott ousted him from between the posts. He was capped eight times by Scotland, winning three of those caps while with Liverpool, and appeared in the 1914 FA Cup final. He later played with New Brighton, Stoke and Leicester City, returning for a second spell with New Brighton in 1929. He retired two years later and opened a sports shop in Wallasey.

CAPACITY. The total capacity of Anfield in 1995 was 42,000. The breakdown was as follows:
Kop: 13,000
Main Stand: 8,771
Paddock: 2,578
Anfield Road End: home supporters 2,392
visitors 3,120
Centenary Stand: lower level 6,809   upper level 4,595

CAPS. The most capped player in the club's history is Emlyn Hughes who won 59 caps for England.

CAPS (ENGLAND). The first Liverpool player to be capped by England was Harry Bradshaw in 1899. The most capped player is Emlyn Hughes.

CAPS (NORTHERN IRELAND). The first Liverpool player to be capped by Northern Ireland was Bill Lacey in 1913. The most capped player is Elisha Scott.

CAPS (SCOTLAND). The first Liverpool player to be capped by Scotland was George Allan in 1897. The most capped player is Kenny Dalglish.

CAPS (THE REPUBLIC OF IRELAND). The first Liverpool player to be capped by the Republic of Ireland was Steve Heighway. The most capped player is Ronnie Whelan.

CAPS (WALES). The first Liverpool player to be capped by Wales was Maurice Parry in 1901. The most capped player is Ian Rush.

CAPTAINS. Among the many players who have captained the club in more recent years have been Ron Yeats, Tommy Smith, Phil Thompson, Graeme Souness, Phil Neal, Alan Hansen, Ronnie Whelan, Steve Nicol, John Barnes and Ian Rush.

CARTER, JIMMY. Young winger signed from Millwall by Kenny Dalglish for £800,000 during the manager's final season with the club. At Millwall Carter had shown some potential but it was not always evident in his few Anfield appearances. The arrival of Graeme Souness at Anfield inevitably spelt the end of his Anfield career and he soon returned to London, joining Arsenal for a fee of £500,000.

CASE, JIMMY. As wholehearted a competitor as you could possibly wish to have in your side, Case was an amateur with

South Liverpool before coming to Anfield in May 1973. Over the next eight years he made well over 200 appearances in the midfield, scoring 45 goals. He liked nothing more than to power into the penalty area like an old-fashioned inside-forward or to hover just outside the box waiting for a loose ball that he could strike. Case had a ferocious shot that produced a number of spectacular goals, including the equaliser against Manchester United in the 1977 FA Cup final. Capped by England at under-23 level, he never represented his country at senior level. But what he missed in international football he more than made up for with a clutch of other honours – three European Cup medals, four league championship medals, a UEFA Cup winners' medal and a few runners-up medals as well. During the summer of 1981 he signed for Brighton in a £350,000 transfer deal and helped them to a Wembley Cup final. He later joined Southampton, playing on well into his 30s and proving that perhaps Liverpool sold him a little prematurely.

Jimmy Case

CELTIC. A strong bond has existed between the Glasgow club and Liverpool over many years. Yet, surprisingly, the two clubs have met only once in competition. That was in 1966 when they faced each other in the semi-final of the European Cup Winners' Cup. Liverpool lost the first leg 0–1 in front of 80,000 at Parkhead but won the return at Anfield 2–0 before a crowd of over 54,000. The two clubs also met to decide the unofficial British championship in Dubai with Celtic winning. There have been a number of friendlies, usually for testimonials, the most notable being at Parkhead for Jock Stein in 1978 and at Anfield for Ron Yeats in 1974. Liverpool also played Celtic shortly after the Hillsborough disaster. Transfer deals have taken place between the two clubs, with the record fee of £440,000 for Kenny Dalglish the most important. In 1995 the two clubs met at Anfield in Ian Rush's testimonial with Liverpool running out 6–0 winners.

CENTENARY. Liverpool celebrated their centenary in 1992.

CENTENARY STAND. The Centenary Stand, formally the Kemlyn Road stand, was officially opened on Tuesday, 1 September 1992, by Lennart Johansson, the president of UEFA. The stand, built during the 1991–92 season, cost just over £8 million. With executive boxes and dining suites, the stand has a capacity for just over 11,000 spectators.

CENTRAL LEAGUE. Now known as the Pontins League. Liverpool have played in the Central League ever since its formation and have won its championship more times than any other club. Between 1969 and 1980 they took the title on ten occasions.

CHADWICK, EDGAR. One of the most famous of all Victorian footballers, Chadwick was well past his prime when he arrived at Anfield in 1902. He had already seen better days with Blackburn Olympic, Blackburn Rovers,

Everton, Burnley and Southampton before he returned north to join Liverpool. Yet he still managed 43 league appearances for the Reds, contributing seven goals before he moved on to Blackpool. He later coached in Holland and Germany. Chadwick, who could play at inside-forward or on the wing, was capped seven times by England, winning all seven while at Everton.

CHAMBERS, HARRY. During the inter-war years Harry Chambers was one of Liverpool's most outstanding players. A goalscorer, playing at either centre-forward or as an inside-forward, Chambers struck at the rate of a goal every other game and was responsible more than any other man for bringing the league title to Anfield twice in the early 1920s. Born near Newcastle, he joined Liverpool during the First World War, although he did not make his league debut until peacetime football resumed in August 1919. He hit 15 league goals that season and over the next few years was to prove a prolific goalscorer. Goals came easily to him despite the bow legs and ungainly style. He had a wicked left-foot shot and could bend the ball as acutely as any modern South American player. The fans knew him as 'Smiler' and in the two championship seasons he managed 41 league goals. In his nine years at Anfield he struck a total of 151 goals in 338 games. In March 1928 Liverpool sold him to West Bromwich Albion. He left Albion a year later but continued playing in non-league football until the grand old age of 52. He was capped eight times by England, scoring five goals.

CHAMPIONSHIP. Liverpool have won the league championship on 18 occasions: 1900–01; 1905–06; 1921–22; 1922–23; 1946–47; 1963–64; 1965–66; 1972–73; 1975–76; 1976–77; 1978–79; 1979–80; 1981–82; 1982–83; 1983–84; 1985–86; 1987–88; 1989–90.

CHAMPIONSHIP – CLOSEST. The league championship of 1988–89 was the closest on record with Liverpool and

Arsenal facing each other at Anfield in a final match of the season decider. Liverpool needed to avoid defeat by two clear goals in order to win not only the championship but also a second double. Victory by two clear goals for Arsenal, however, would take the title to Highbury. In the event Arsenal won 2–0 with a goal in injury time and thereby took the championship. Although both sides had equal points and equal goal difference, Arsenal had scored more goals than Liverpool. On the old goal average system Liverpool would have been champions.

CHAMPIONSHIP – TREBLE. Between 1981 and 1984 Liverpool won the championship three consecutive years, thereby emulating the feat Huddersfield Town and Arsenal achieved during the 1920s and 1930s.

CHARITY SHIELD. Liverpool have appeared in more Charity Shield games than any other club – a total of 18 – and have also won the pre-season friendly on more occasions than anyone else:

1922 v Huddersfield Town (Old Trafford) 0–1
1964 v West Ham United (Anfield) 2–2
1965 v Manchester United (Old Trafford) 2–2
1966 v Everton (Goodison Park) 1–0
1971 v Leicester (Filbert Street) 0–1
1974 v Leeds (Wembley) 1–1 (Liverpool won 6–5 on penalties)
1976 v Southampton (Wembley) 1–0
1977 v Manchester United (Wembley) 0–0
1979 v Arsenal (Wembley) 3–1
1980 v West Ham (Wembley) 1–0
1982 v Tottenham (Wembley) 1–0
1983 v Manchester United (Wembley) 0–2
1984 v Everton (Wembley) 0–1
1986 v Everton (Wembley) 1–1
1988 v Wimbledon (Wembley) 2–1
1989 v Arsenal (Wembley) 1–0

1990 v Manchester United (Wembley) 1–1
1992 v Leeds (Wembley) 3–4
Liverpool also appeared in the 1906 game, beating Corinthians 5–1, when the competition was known as the Sheriff of London's Charity Shield.

CHISNALL, PHIL. One of the few players in post-war football to have been transferred between Manchester United and Liverpool, Chisnall, an England schoolboy star, joined United from his Manchester school in 1958. He played 47 games for United and scored ten goals when Bill Shankly swooped to sign him in April 1964 for £25,000. But it never worked out and after just six league appearances in three years, Chisnall was sold to Southend for £12,000.

CLEMENCE, RAY. A typical Shankly signing, Clemence was picked up from Scunthorpe in the lower divisions for a mere £18,000 in June 1967. He broke into the first team towards the end of the 1969–70 season, but once he had taken up position there was no removing him and he was to be ever present over the next ten seasons. He eventually played 656 games for the club before Liverpool sold him to Tottenham Hotspur for £300,000 in April 1981. Tall, slim and agile, Clemence was an outstanding 'keeper in an era of great names. Quick off the line, fast and with a natural spring, he helped turn goalkeeping into a new science. He won 56 England caps while at Anfield and collected a total of 61 for his country. Yet without the likes of Shilton around he would undoubtedly have collected many more. Clemence retired in April 1988 but then went on to hold various coaching positions with Spurs. At Anfield he had collected just about every honour in the game, including three European Cup medals, two UEFA medals, five championships, an FA Cup winners' medal and a League Cup medal. He was also awarded the MBE.

CLOUGH, NIGEL. England international signed from Nottingham Forest during the summer of 1993 for £2m.

Ray Clemence

The son of the former Forest manager, Brian Clough, he played more than 300 games for Forest, scoring over 100 goals. He scored twice on his Liverpool league debut against Sheffield Wednesday. Unfortunately that was to be the highlight of his Anfield career. He was never a regular under Graeme Souness and has made even fewer appearances since Roy Evans took over although he has frequently been named as substitute.

COACHES. One of the most famous coaches in the club's history was the former Liverpool player Charlie Wilson who captained the team to their first ever league title in 1901. He later became one of the club's first coaches, serving in various capacities until the outbreak of the Second World War. In more recent years those on the coaching staff have included Reuben Bennett, Bob Paisley, Joe Fagan, Ronnie Moran, Roy Evans, Phil Thompson, Phil Boersma and Sammy Lee.

COCA-COLA CUP. See **FOOTBALL LEAGUE CUP.**

COHEN, AVI. Israeli-born defender who promised much but with so many other outstanding defenders at Anfield never really had the opportunity to show his worth. He joined Liverpool from the Israeli club Macabbi, after a trial period, in the spring of 1979 for £200,000, but over the next two years made only 16 league appearances. Tall and calm, he seemed just a mite too relaxed at times though he often brought an air of dispassion to the Liverpool defence when it was most needed. Having put into his own net against Aston Villa at the end of the 1979-80 season in the game that would give Liverpool the title, he later raced upfield and scored to put Liverpool ahead. It was typical of Cohen and it was disappointing that he was never given the chance to develop his range of talents. When Graeme Souness became the Rangers manager one of his first signings was Cohen. He was already an Israeli international when he arrived at Anfield and went on to win many more caps.

COLLYMORE, STAN. Signed by Roy Evans in the summer of 1995 from Nottingham Forest for a British transfer record fee of £8.5 million. Two years earlier Forest had signed him from Southend United for £2.2 million. It was a nice profit for Forest although they really wanted to keep their man. Collymore began his football with Stafford Rangers and in December 1990 moved to Crystal Palace for £100,000. Unfortunately he did not get too many chances at Palace and two years later dropped down the divisions to Southend United where he suddenly began to fulfil his potential. The goals began to flow but Forest were the only Premiership club tempted to give him a try in the top division. It paid dividends with 50 goals in his two seasons at Forest, making him one of the top marksmen in the country. It was also enough to persuade Terry Venables to give him his first England cap during the summer of 1995.

COLOURS. During their early years Liverpool played in white shirts with a red V around the neck. They changed to the now familiar red shirt after just a few years. For the European Cup-tie against Anderlecht in 1965 Bill Shankly decided to try the team in red shorts as well as their red shirts. But the intention was that they keep the white socks. However, Ron Yeats and Ian St John persuaded Shankly to try red socks as well. Shankly was so impressed by the fearsome sight of Ron Yeats in the all-red strip that he agreed to let them wear the red stockings as well.

CONSECUTIVE SCORING – LONGEST SEQUENCE. John Aldridge holds the Football League record for consecutive scoring when he was on target in ten consecutive games. His first came in the final match of the 1986–87 season and was followed by nine consecutive strikes from the start of the next season.

COOPER, TOM. One of the finest defenders of the inter-war years, Cooper had been capped 15 times by England

Stan Collymore

and had even captained his country when he joined Liverpool from Derby County in December 1934 for £7,500. It was a hefty fee but Cooper, then 30 years old, was worth every penny. Over the next five seasons until the outbreak of war he played 160 games for the Reds and was appointed club captain. A resourceful, scheming full-back, Cooper made up for his lack of height with guile and pace. During the war he joined the military police but was sadly killed in a motor-bike accident in June 1940.

Tom Cooper

CORMACK, PETER. Bill Shankly reckoned Peter Cormack one of the most elegant half-backs he had ever seen. He was a delight to watch with his certain first touch and accurate passing. He joined the club from Nottingham Forest in July 1972 for a fee of £110,000. Already a Scottish international with nine caps to his credit from his days at Hibernian and Forest, Cormack went on to make 168 appearances for Liverpool, scoring 26 goals though surprisingly adding no more international honours to his collection. He had begun his career as an old-fashioned inside-forward but as styles changed he switched to the midfield. He had a swanky, refined look about him, bringing pace and thought to the Liverpool team of the early 1970s. The emergence of Ray Kennedy threatened his position, however, and in November 1976 he was sold to Bristol City. He ended his playing days with his former club Hibernian and then had four years as manager of Partick Thistle.

COX, JACK. Began life as an outside-right but really found fame as an outside-left where he won three England caps. He joined Liverpool from Blackpool in 1898 and enjoyed 12 seasons at Anfield, playing 360 games, scoring 80 goals.

CRICKET. A number of Liverpool players have also played first-class cricket. They include Harry Storer who played six games for Derbyshire in 1895 and Gordon Hodgson, the South African who also turned out for Lancashire.

CUNLIFFE, DAN. An outstanding Victorian inside-forward who joined Liverpool during the summer of 1897, he had just one year at the club, playing a mere 14 games at inside-right and scoring six goals. He left to join the newly created New Brighton Tower in 1888 but a year after that was on the move again, this time to Portsmouth where he was to enjoy his finest days, winning an England cap. He came back to New Brighton Tower the following year but when the Wallasey club folded he returned to Portsmouth.

CUPS. In its long history the club has won 34 major trophies. They are:
18 League titles; 5 FA Cups; 5 League Cups; 4 European Cups; 2 UEFA Cups; In addition they have also won the European Super Cup and numerous Charity Shields.

D

DALGLISH, KENNY. The Scottish international striker joined Liverpool from Glasgow Celtic in August 1977 for a British record fee of £440,000 and made his first appearance for Liverpool at Wembley a few days later in the Charity Shield. It was to be the first of more than 480 appearances for the club. Dalglish will go down as one of the finest ever players to wear the red shirt. His ability to hold the ball and turn was a revelation and his later partnership with Ian Rush proved to be the most lethal in the first division. At the end of his first season he scored the winning goal in the European Cup final against Bruges to make Liverpool the first British team ever to win two European Cups. It was to be the start of a glittering career at Anfield. By the time he left he had won five league championships, three European Cups, four League Cups and had scored 168 goals. By then he was probably the most honoured player in British soccer history. At Celtic he had also won five League titles, four Scottish Cups and one Scottish League Cup, scoring more than 100 goals. On the eve of Liverpool's ill-fated European Cup final against Juventus in 1985 he was surprisingly appointed player-manager, the first ever player-manager in the club's long history. But it was clearly an

Kenny Dalglish

inspired decision. In his first season in charge Liverpool clinched the Double. During his managerial reign he added two more league titles to his collection and two FA Cups. And on two occasions he came within a whisker of pulling off the Double again. Under Dalglish Liverpool cast aside the committed style that had won them so many honours and with new signings John Barnes and Peter Beardsley instead developed a flair and excitement rarely associated with the club. His dealings in the transfer market showed that he also had an astute eye for a good player, with the signings of Ray Houghton, John Aldridge, Ronnie Rosenthal and David Burrows as well as youngsters such as Jamie Redknapp and Don Hutchison. In February 1991 Dalglish surprisingly resigned as manager of Liverpool, claiming that the pressures had been too great. After a nine-month lay-off he took over at Blackburn Rovers and in his first season steered the second division side into the Premier League. Capped on a record 102 occasions by Scotland, Dalglish also scored a record 30 goals for his country and played in three World Cup finals. Unfortunately, at an international level he only too rarely demonstrated his wide range of skills. He was Footballer of the Year twice, PFA Player of the Year and has been Manager of the Year on three occasions. He is also an MBE. In 1995 Blackburn Rovers won the Premiership title under his guidance and he was again named Manager of the Year. He is only the third manager this century to have managed two different clubs to the league title. In June 1995 he stepped down as team manager at Blackburn to become director of football at Ewood Park.

DEFEAT – WORST. Liverpool's record defeat was when Birmingham City beat them 9–1 in a second division game on 11 December 1954 at St Andrews. In 1934 they also conceded nine goals as Newcastle beat them 9–2 at St James Park. Liverpool's worst home defeat was in April 1930 when Sunderland won 6–0 at Anfield. Later that year, in December, Sunderland put another six past Liverpool, this time at Roker Park, although Liverpool did manage five in return.

DEFEATS – FEWEST. During the 1893–94 season Liverpool went an entire season without defeat, winning 22 of their 28 games and drawing the remainder. During the 1987–88 season Liverpool were beaten only twice, by Everton and Nottingham Forest, to equal Leeds United's record for the first division.

DEFEATS – MOST. Liverpool's total of 23 defeats during the 1953–54 season is the worst in the club's history. Not surprisingly, they were relegated at the end of the season.

DEFENSIVE RECORDS – BEST. Liverpool won the 1978–79 championship, conceding a mere 16 goals in 42 games. They conceded only seven in their last 21 games. Their goal difference of 69 is also a first division record.

DERBIES. The first Liverpool-Everton derby took place on 13 October 1893 at Goodison Park. It was Liverpool's opening season in the first division and they took the game so seriously that they went off to Hightown for a week's training, whereas Everton remained at home. But it made little difference. Watched by a crowd of 44,000, including the Lord Mayor and other city dignitaries, Everton went on to win 3–0. In the return game at Anfield the following month Liverpool managed a better result, drawing 2–2, in front of a crowd of 26,000. Since then the two clubs have met many times in the league. In September 1935 Liverpool had a memorable 6–0 win over Everton at Anfield and in November 1982 won 5–0 at Goodison. The two clubs have also met on a number of occasions in the FA Cup, the most famous being their Cup final meeting in 1986 when a 3–1 win for Liverpool clinched the Double. Three seasons later they again met at Wembley with Liverpool winning 3–2 after extra time. Another famous Cup meeting came in 1950 when the two sides met in the semi-final at Maine Road, Liverpool winning 2–0 thanks to a goal by Bob Paisley. The two clubs also met in the League Cup final in 1984. It was the first time they had met in a final with the first game at Wembley ending in a goalless draw. Four days later at Maine Road Liverpool won 1–0. Perhaps the most astonishing derby result was in January 1955 when the two clubs met in the fourth round of the FA Cup at Goodison. Everton were possibly the hottest ever favourites to win a derby. They were in seventh spot in the first division while Liverpool were lying in the bottom half of the second. In the event Liverpool won 4–0.

DEVLIN, WILLIAM. Sometimes known as 'Demon' Devlin for his goalscoring feats. During three seasons between 1923 and 1926 with Cowdenbeath Devlin struck 99 goals. He was soon spotted by Huddersfield Town who brought him to Leeds Road for what was then a huge transfer fee of £4,200. But in a star-filled Huddersfield side Devlin lasted little more than a year and was transferred to Liverpool in May 1927 for a knockdown price. But he failed to settle and after just 19 appearances, in which he scored a creditable 15 goals, he went back to Scotland, joining Hearts. He later played for a number of non-league sides and finally ended up with Olympique Marseille in France.

DICKS, JULIAN. Full-back signed by manager Graeme Souness in September 1993 in an exchange deal that took Mike Marsh and David Burrows to West Ham United. Although no money changed hands Dicks' value was estimated at £1.6 million. Liverpool fans were shocked by the deal, especially given Dicks' disciplinary record. Dicks never really looked comfortable in the Liverpool defence and following the departure of Souness, he returned to West Ham.

DINES, JOE. Although Joe Dines made only one league appearance for Liverpool he deserves mention because he was an Olympic gold medallist, having been a member of the 1912 Great Britain Olympic soccer winning side. Dines was a left-half who joined the club in 1912. A teacher by profession, he was killed on the Western Front during the First World War.

DOHERTY, PETER. Although the famous Irish international was never on Liverpool's books, he once guested for the club against Blackpool in February 1942. Doherty had turned up in the Liverpool dressing-room at Bloomfield Road shortly before kick-off to chat with some of his footballing colleagues. When George Kay, the Liverpool manager, spotted him he asked him if he would like a game. And so Doherty was enlisted. But the presence of the great man made little difference; Liverpool were trounced 6–2. Unfortunately Doherty's appearance was to land Liverpool in trouble as they had already arranged for George Ainsley of Leeds to guest with them. This meant that Ainsley's journey had been wasted after they had organised leave of absence from the RAF. The authorities did not look upon it kindly and Liverpool were severely reprimanded by the RAF and forced to apologise.

DOIG, NED. The first of Liverpool's great goalkeepers. Born in Forfar in October 1866, he began his career with Arbroath in 1883. He then signed for Blackburn Rovers but made only one appearance before joining Sunderland where he came under the careful guidance of manager Tom Watson. Doig was to become a distinguished goalkeeper with Sunderland in what was an outstanding side, first division champions on four occasions in ten years. During this spell he also won seven Scottish caps. Doig eventually joined his former manager, Tom Watson, by then at Liverpool, in 1904, and remained with the club until 1908, making 51 appearances. He played eight games during Liverpool's championship-winning season of 1905–06 and had been ever-present the previous season as Liverpool clinched the second division title, conceding just 25 goals. He kept a clean sheet on 16 occasions that season. He eventually retired in 1908, handing over to another fine goalkeeper, Sam Hardy.

DONE, CYRIL. Cyril Done was one of many Liverpool players who probably missed their best days through war. A centre-forward, he made his debut for Liverpool on 2 September 1939, the day before war broke out and even scored in Liverpool's 1–0 win over Chelsea at Anfield. But it was also to be the last league game he would play for seven years. When peace returned he was almost 27 but he did make 17 appearances as Liverpool captured the league title during that first post-war season, 1946–47. During the war he had been a prolific scorer but after the war his scoring instinct seemed to leave him, though he would still score 37 goals in a total of 109 games over the next six years. He eventually crossed the Mersey, signing for Tranmere Rovers in 1952, and later joined Port Vale, making just one appearance when he scored four goals in their 4–3 win over Liverpool. He died in February 1993.

DONE, ROBERT. Half-back who came to Liverpool from Runcorn just days before the 1926 General Strike broke out. He left nine years later, joining Reading. By then he had played almost 150 league games, scoring 13 goals, most of them from the penalty spot.

DOUBLE. In 1986 Liverpool became only the third club this century to clinch the coveted league and FA Cup double. It was not, however, the first time that they had won two major trophies in a season:
1972–3 League and UEFA Cup; 1975–76 League and UEFA Cup; 1976–77 League and European Cup; 1980–81 European Cup and League Cup; 1981–82 League and League Cup; 1982–83 League and League Cup; 1983–84 League, European Cup and League Cup; 1985–86 League and FA Cup.

DUNLOP, WILLIAM. In his 15 years at Anfield at the turn

of the century Billy Dunlop clocked up over 300 league appearances. He made his debut in 1895 as a left-back and held on to that spot until 1909, during which time Liverpool won two league titles and two second division titles. Born in Kilmarnock, he wound up as assistant trainer at Sunderland.

DYNAMO TBILISI. The Georgian side inflicted one of Liverpool's heaviest ever defeats on them in European competition when they beat the Reds 3–0 in front of a crowd of 80,000 in the Soviet Union. In the first-leg the skilful Georgians had gone down 2–1 at Anfield.

E

EDMED, DICK. Played for Liverpool between 1926 and 1932. An outside-right, he joined the club from Gillingham for £1,800 where he had created something of a sensation with his speed and goals. Edmed was a useful asset at Anfield, forming a powerful partnership with Gordon Hodgson and netting 46 goals over his five seasons, scoring 16 league goals during the 1928–29 season. A cartilage injury finally took its toll and at the end of the 1931 season he was transferred to Bolton Wanderers. He had just two seasons at Burnden Park when injury finally forced early retirement. He played just once during the first season but managed to get on the score sheet as Bolton thrashed Liverpool 8–1 in the final league game of the season.

EIRE. The first Liverpool player to be capped by the Republic of Ireland was Steve Heighway when he played against Poland in 1971. The most capped Irish player in Liverpool's history is Ronnie Whelan, who has won more than 50 caps playing for his country.

ENGLAND. The first Liverpool player to be capped by England was Harry Bradshaw who played for England against Ireland at Nottingham on 20 February 1897. England won 6–0. The Liverpool player to win the most England caps is Emlyn Hughes, who made 59 appearances for his country while a Liverpool player. In September 1977 six Liverpool players lined up for England against Switzerland at Wembley. They were Ian Callaghan, Terry McDermott, Ray Clemence, Phil Neal, Ray Kennedy and captain Emlyn Hughes. Kevin Keegan, transferred from Liverpool to Hamburg the previous month, also played.

ENGLISH, SAM. Won fame as a Glasgow Rangers striker though, sadly, he is remembered more for the tragic accident he was involved in than for his goals. Playing for Rangers against Celtic in 1931, English chased a loose ball into the penalty area only to collide with John Thompson, the famous Celtic and Scotland goalkeeper, as he raced off his goal-line and dived bravely at English's feet. Thompson, a legend in his time, sustained serious injuries and died later that night in hospital from a fractured skull. English was never forgiven by one half of Glasgow, especially as he went on to break the Rangers' scoring record with 44 goals that season. After another year at Ibrox he decided it would be best to leave Scotland and signed for Liverpool in August 1933 for £8,000. He had a reasonably successful early spell at Anfield, scoring 21 goals in 31 appearances in this first season. After that the goals seemed to dry up and, with only six goals the following season, he was transferred to Queen of the South in July 1935. Perhaps the problem was partly due to the barracking from the terraces which followed him wherever he went. Yet English was totally blameless for his part in the death of Thompson. Even Thompson's Celtic team-mates came to his defence. In the cold hatred of Glasgow football, however, the diehard fans of the terraces viewed it differently. Born in Coleraine, English was a Northern Ireland international, capped twice while at Rangers.

EUROPEAN CUP. Liverpool have been winners of Europe's

premier trophy on four occasions, a feat bettered only by Real Madrid. Liverpool first entered the competition during the 1964–65 season, reaching the semi-finals. They first won the trophy in 1977, overpowering Borussia Moenchengladbach 3–1 in the Olympic stadium in Rome. The following year they retained their trophy, beating Bruges 1–0 at Wembley. In 1981 they again lifted the European Cup, this time overcoming Real Madrid by a single goal in Paris. But perhaps Liverpool's most dramatic victory was in 1984 when they won on penalties after a 1–1 draw against Roma, again in Rome's Olympic stadium. The following year Liverpool reached the final for the fifth time but were beaten 1–0 by Juventus in the Heysel stadium.

EUROPEAN CUP WINNERS' CUP. This is the one European trophy to have eluded Liverpool. The club made its debut in the competition in 1965 and went on to reach the final where they were beaten 2–1 by Borussia Dortmund at Hampden Park after extra time. Since then Liverpool have made three more appearances in the competition but with little success.

EUROPEAN SUPER CUP. Liverpool's three appearances in this competition, played between the European Cup holders and the winners of the European Cup Winners' Cup, have brought mixed fortunes. On their first appearance in 1977 Liverpool lifted the trophy, beating Hamburg 7–1 over two legs. A year later they lost 3–4 to Anderlecht. In 1985 the competition was played as a one-off game, with Juventus winning 2–0 in Turin.

EVANS, ALUN. The most expensive teenager in English football history when Bill Shankly signed him for £100,000 in September 1968 from Wolves. He was then just 18 years old. His Anfield career began well with a debut goal but his promise never quite materialised. He was involved in a brawl one evening in a nightclub and was badly cut about the face, injuries which seemed to seriously undermine his

European Cup programme 1977

European Cup 1977

European Cup 1978

European Cup 1984

confidence. He also had a cartilage injury which interrupted his comeback. He was never quite the same and after just four seasons at Anfield he was transferred to Aston Villa in June 1972 for £70,000. Fast and dangerous, many, including Shankly, expected Evans to become one of the game's leading players. In the end it was a salutary lesson in the vagaries of football. Evans, however, will always be fondly remembered for a stunning hat trick he scored against Bayern Munich at Anfield when his powerful running left Beckenbauer and company chasing shadows. Capped at Under-23 level.

EVANS, JOHN. John Evans' main claim to fame was as the scorer of all five Liverpool goals in the club's 5–3 win over Bristol Rovers in September 1954. Evans was a useful goalscorer, netting 49 league goals in 96 appearances during the 1950s, but it was never enough to take Liverpool out of the second division. He came to Anfield from Charlton Athletic in 1953 for £12,500, a high fee in those days. But with second division football looming at that point Liverpool were desperate. He played for the Football League in their 3–2 defeat by the Scottish League at Hampden Park in March 1955 and left to join Colchester in 1957.

EVANS, ROY. Came to Anfield from school in Bootle, making his debut at full-back in 1970. His appearances were few and far between, just 11 in nine playing seasons, and in 1974, at the age of 25, he hung up his boots to take over as coach to the reserves. He was to prove extraordinarily successful in his new job, leading the reserves to numerous titles. At the end of the 1992–93 season he was appointed assistant manager to Graeme Souness and eventually took over as manager when Souness was sacked in January 1994. For the remainder of that season he bided his time but during the 1994–95 season he made changes and his side began to take shape. Multi-million pound signings Phil Babb and John Scales proved inspired and by the end of the season Evans had won his first trophy as manager when

Liverpool lifted the Coca-Cola Cup. Thoughtful and unassuming Evans is highly regarded at Anfield and has played an important part in Liverpool's many successes over the years.

EVERTON. Liverpool Football Club really began life as Everton Football Club. Everton had been founded in 1878 as St Domingo's, changing its name a year later to Everton. During the 1880s Everton came to the attention of a prominent local businessman and politician, John Houlding, who helped find a new home for the club at Anfield. And so in September 1884 Everton began to play their games at the present Anfield ground. They were admitted to the Football League in 1888 and two years later were champions for the first time. But then in 1892 a backroom row over the amount of rent to be paid for Anfield led to the team and its officials storming out of Anfield. The club quickly found a new home for itself at Goodison Park while Anfield was left empty with its owners furious. So, John Houlding decided that he would try and create a new football team to play at Anfield. Initially he wanted to continue calling it Everton. But the old Everton continued to play under that name. So, Houlding decided to call his club Liverpool. Eleven players were soon recruited and in May 1892 the club officially began life. Since then the fortunes of the two clubs have been inextricably entwined.

F

FA CUP. Liverpool first participated in the FA Cup in October 1892, making their debut at Nantwich where they won 4–0. Since then they have gone on to win the trophy on five occasions. Their first appearance in a final was in 1914 when they were beaten by Burnley at the Crystal Palace.

FA CUP FINALS. Liverpool have appeared in ten FA Cup finals, winning the trophy on five occasions:
1914 v Burnley (Crystal Palace) 0–1
1950 v Arsenal (Wembley) 0–2
1965 v Leeds (Wembley) 2–1 *aet*
1971 v Arsenal (Wembley) 1–2 *aet*
1974 v Newcastle (Wembley) 3–0
1977 v Manchester United (Wembley) 1–2
1986 v Everton (Wembley) 3–1
1988 v Wimbledon (Wembley) 0–1
1989 v Everton (Wembley) 3–2 *aet*
1992 v Sunderland (Wembley) 2–0

FA CUP SEMI-FINALS. Liverpool have participated in 19 FA Cup semi-finals up to the end of the 1992–93 season.

FAGAN, JOE. It was ironic that the Liverpool-born Joe Fagan should escape the clutches of the two Merseyside giants, only to return years later and lead Liverpool to numerous honours as coach and manager. Fagan's playing career began instead in Manchester at Maine Road but was immediately interrupted by war. After hostilities he made 158 appearances in the light blue shirt and then had spells with Nelson, Bradford Park Avenue and Rochdale before moving to Anfield to join Bill Shankly's coaching staff. When Paisley took over from Shankly, Fagan moved up a notch and when Paisley retired in 1983 Joe Fagan was the automatic choice as manager. He began with a young side that had little trouble in retaining the league title during his first season, Liverpool's third successive championship. That season they also lifted the European Cup as well as the Milk Cup. Three trophies in his first season was a hard act to follow and the next season proved a bitter disappointment. Liverpool wound up second in the league, behind Everton, and were knocked out of the Cup in the semi-finals by Manchester United. Yet there seemed every hope that Liverpool would lift the European Cup for a fifth time: instead, on a tragic night in Brussels, Fagan's career ended in horror. Having announced his retirement that day, this was his last game as manager. Fagan's two years in charge had taken their toll; he was a tired man, already over 60 when he took over as manager. During those years he brought many new faces to Anfield, including John Wark, Michael Robinson and Paul Walsh, and gave debuts to Jim Beglin and Jan Molby. Fagan had been at Anfield for more than 30 years when he retired and it was sad that his career had to end on such an unhappy note.

FAGAN, WILLIE. Willie Fagan was a much travelled player. Born in Musselburgh in Scotland, he began his footballing days with Celtic but travelled south to join Preston North End in 1936. A year later he came to Liverpool. He was a powerful, bustling inside-forward, though equally at home leading the attack, who would undoubtedly have gone on to

Joe Fagan

score many more goals had it not been for the outbreak of war. As it was he was barely 22 years old when hostilities began. During the war he guested for a host of clubs, including Newcastle, Chelsea, Millwall, Reading and half a dozen more. At the end of the war he returned to Anfield and was a member of the championship side of 1946–47, netting seven goals in 18 matches. But his appearances were becoming less frequent and in 1952 he joined Weymouth as player-manager, having scored 57 goals in 185 appearances for Liverpool. He also played a number of wartime internationals for Scotland and played for Preston in the 1937 Cup final. He was in the Liverpool side that was beaten by Arsenal at Wembley in the 1950 Cup final.

FAIRCLOUGH, DAVID. Better known as 'Super Sub'. A Liverpool lad, Fairclough joined the club directly from school in 1974 and played a major role in Liverpool's assault on Europe. He made his league debut in November 1975 and went on to notch up 64 appearances (36 of these as substitute) and to score 34 goals. His greatest moment came against St Étienne in the 1977 quarter-final of the European Cup when he came on as substitute late in the second half at Anfield to fire Liverpool into the semi-final. He was used with considerable effect by Liverpool, pulling off his track suit to appear for the last 15 minutes or so of a game. And on countless occasions it proved successful as he either scored or laid on a winning goal. The appearance of Fairclough seemed to act as a lucky omen or at the very least to terrify the opposition. Tall, gangly and carrot-haired, Fairclough was unmistakable. He was quick and dangerous, prepared to run at defences and carry the ball into the penalty area. It was difficult to shake him off the ball and he had a knack of being in the right scoring place at the right time. And yet despite his many attributes he really had only one season as a Liverpool regular. In most of his seven playing years at Anfield he appeared only occasionally, with half of his games as substitute. He somehow never seemed quite as dangerous when he started a match and once his Super Sub threat had worn off Liverpool decided to let him go. He initially went to Canada and then played for the Swiss club Basle before returning to England.

FAIRFOUL, TOM. Scottish-born right-half who was suspended in 1915 for his part in the betting scandal that rocked Edwardian football. Fairfoul, born in 1881, joined Third Lanark in 1906 where he became a seasoned campaigner. He moved to Liverpool in 1913 and was immediately drafted into the first team where he proved a resounding success, appearing in the 1914 Cup final. A sturdy and sure half-back, Fairfoul played in the Good Friday 1915 game against Manchester United where a betting ring was found to have operated to rig the result. Fairfoul was one of a number of United and Liverpool players found guilty of conspiring to fix the result and he was suspended *sine die* by the Football League. As it was, war intervened, the league was suspended and Fairfoul anyhow was already 34. It was the end of his career.

FAIRS CUP. This European competition, now known as the UEFA Cup, began its life in 1955 as the Industrial Fairs Cup. A team representing London were England's first participants, beaten 8–2 on aggregate by Barcelona in the final. Liverpool participated in the old Fairs Cup on four occasions, first during the 1967–68 season when they were knocked out by Ferencvaros in the third round. The following season they were eliminated in the first round by Atletico Bilbao. The next year they managed one round better until Vitoria Setubal of Portugal overcame them. A year later Liverpool's growing European experience finally began to tell as they reached the semi-final, only to lose narrowly to Leeds United.

FAMILIES. Among the families who have played for Liverpool are the two Goldie brothers Archie and William, who played for the club before the turn of the century.

Liverpool has also boasted a number of father and son players, the most notable being Roy Saunders and his son Dean. There is also a grandfather and grandson with Bill Jones who played for the club between 1938 and 1954 and the current full-back Rob Jones.

FERGUSON, ROBERT. Pre-First World War centre-half who joined Liverpool from Third Lanark. He played in Liverpool's FA Cup final side of 1914 but never returned to football after the war. Ferguson notched up 92 league appearances for Liverpool.

FEWEST DEFEATS. During 1893–94 Liverpool went the entire season in the second division without defeat – a total of 28 games, which remains a Football League record. Liverpool did hold the record, along with Leeds United, for the fewest defeats this century in the first division. During the 1987–88 season they lost just two games, to Everton and Nottingham Forest. This record was beaten by Arsenal who lost just one game during the 1990–91 season.

FLOODLIGHTS. Anfield switched on its floodlights for the first time on 30 October 1957 with a friendly against Everton to commemorate the 75th anniversary of the Liverpool County FA. Liverpool won 3–2. The lights, which had cost £12,000, were originally on four small pylons erected in each corner of the ground. European football rules, however, later insisted that more powerful lights were needed and in 1973 new lights were installed on the roof of the new Main Stand and the Kemlyn Road Stand. When a second tier was added to the Kemlyn Road Stand in 1992, new lights were erected on top of the new stand, now called the Centenary Stand.

FOOTBALL LEAGUE. Liverpool joined the second division of the Football League in 1893 after one year in the Lancashire League. 1993 marked 100 years of league football for Liverpool FC.

FOOTBALL LEAGUE CUP. For a time Liverpool did not appear interested in the Football League Cup and even failed to participate during its early years. But once the final was booked for Wembley their interest began to grow, although it still took some years before they finally lifted football's newest trophy. But once they had won it they went on to set a record of four consecutive wins. In a ten-year spell between 1978 and 1987 Liverpool reached the semi-finals on eight occasions. Liverpool first participated in the League Cup in October 1960, kicking off with a 1–1 draw at Anfield against Luton. In 1982 the trophy was renamed the Milk Cup and has subsequently been known as the Littlewoods Cup and the Rumbelows Cup. It is currently called the Coca Cola Cup. Liverpool have now won the trophy on five occasions, appearing in seven finals.

Final Appearances:

1978 Nottingham Forest 0 Liverpool 0 (*aet*) Wembley
      Nottingham Forest 1 Liverpool 0 Old Trafford
1981 Liverpool 1 West Ham United 1 (*aet*) Wembley
      Liverpool 2 West Ham United 1 Villa Park
1982 Liverpool 3 Tottenham 1 (*aet*) Wembley
1983 Liverpool 2 Manchester United 1 (*aet*) Wembley
1984 Liverpool 0 Everton 0 (*aet*) Wembley
      Liverpool 1 Everton 0 Maine Road
1987 Arsenal 2 Liverpool 1 Wembley
1995 Liverpool 2 Bolton Wanderers 1 Wembley

FOOTBALLER OF THE YEAR. The Football Writers' Footballer of the Year award has been won by Liverpool players on a number of occasions. Past winners have been:

1974 Ian Callaghan
1976 Kevin Keegan
1977 Emlyn Hughes
1979 Kenny Dalglish
1980 Terry McDermott
1983 Kenny Dalglish
1984 Ian Rush

1988 John Barnes
1989 Steve Nicol
1990 John Barnes
The Professional Football Association award for Player of the Year has also gone to a number of Liverpool players.
1980 Terry McDermott
1983 Kenny Dalglish
1984 Ian Rush
1988 John Barnes
In 1995 Robbie Fowler was named Young Player of the Year.

FORSHAW, DICK. Inside-forward Dick Forshaw was a vital cog in the Liverpool side that lifted two championships in the early 1920s. He scored 36 goals over the two title seasons and was a brilliant foil for centre-forward Harry Chambers. Forshaw came to Anfield in 1919 after wartime spells as a guest with Nottingham Forest and Middlesbrough and was soon a regular first-teamer. Over the next eight seasons he made 266 appearances, scoring 117 goals, and was then surprisingly sold to Everton. It turned out to be Liverpool's loss as Forshaw went on to win a third championship medal.

FOWLER, ROBBIE. Liverpool striker. Broke into the Liverpool side under manager Graeme Souness, making his debut against Fulham in the League Cup in September 1993. At the age of 18, he was one of the youngest debutants in the club's history. Scored on his debut and a couple of weeks later in the return leg bagged five goals. Few players in the history of the game have had as dramatic a start as Fowler. By the end of his first season, in which he played 33 games, he had scored 17 goals. The following season he was even more devastating in the penalty area hitting 25 league goals to make him the second highest marksman in the Premiership. He also managed six in other competitions. Since then he has picked up England Under-21 honours, B international honours – even scoring on his

Robbie Fowler

debut – and was named for the full England squad. Fowler is rated by many at Liverpool as one of the finest prospects for years. Born in Toxteth in Liverpool in 1975 he has already been a winner at Wembley in the Coca-Cola Cup and was named PFA Young Player of the Year in 1995.

FURNELL, JIM. Born in Clitheroe, Furnell began his playing days with Burnley but with so much goalkeeping talent at Turf Moor he was transferred to Liverpool in February 1962 for £18,000. He immediately took over from Bert Slater in the Liverpool goal and although he showed early promise as Liverpool clinched the second division title, by November 1962 he had made way for Tommy Lawrence. After that Furnell was always the second string choice, making only the occasional appearance. He eventually decided to try his luck elsewhere and in November 1963 moved to Arsenal for £15,000. He made more than 150 appearances for the Gunners. He later played for Rotherham and Plymouth Argyle, and was assistant manager at Blackburn Rovers in the early 1980s.

G

GAYLE, HOWARD. Howard Gayle's moment of glory came in the semi-finals of the European Cup in April 1981 when he came on as substitute for Kenny Dalglish, and ran the Bayern Munich defence ragged. But while many thought he might have been rewarded with a regular place in the side, Gayle was instead discarded. Although he was at Anfield for six years he made just three league appearances before joining Birmingham City in January 1985 for £75,000. A Liverpool lad, he was also the club's first black player.

GEARY, FRED. Was one of Everton's finest ever strikers, scoring 86 goals in just 98 appearances. He was transferred to Liverpool in 1895 for £60 but by then was already in the twilight of his career and never had quite the same impact. However he did manage 14 goals in 40 appearances and helped Liverpool to the second division championship in 1896. He retired in 1899. He collected championship honours with Everton in 1891 when the club still played at Anfield, plus two England caps.

GERHADI, HUGH. South African Hugh Gerhadi's main

claim to fame is that at 6ft 4in he is probably the tallest outfield player Liverpool have ever had. He joined the club in 1952 but after just six league appearances returned to South Africa the following year.

GIANTKILLERS. A club of Liverpool's size could never claim the title of having been giantkillers, but one or two other teams could claim that honour after taking Liverpool's scalp. Perhaps the worst defeat in the club's history came in January 1959 when non-league Worcester City beat Liverpool – then in the second division – 2–1 at Worcester in the third round of the FA Cup. There was another humiliation for Liverpool in 1993 when Bolton Wanderers, two divisions lower than Liverpool, came to Anfield for a third round FA Cup replay and won 2–0. At the time Liverpool were the Cup holders. The previous season had also seen something of an embarrassment when Liverpool went to Peterborough in the fourth round of the Rumbelows Cup and lost 1–0. In 1994 Liverpool suffered another humiliation when they were beaten 1–0 at Anfield by Bristol City in the third round of the FA Cup.

GILLESPIE, GARY. Arrived from Coventry for £325,000 in July 1983 and was sold to Glasgow Celtic in the summer of 1991 for £1 million. During his years at Liverpool Gillespie won a couple of championship medals and numerous runners-up medals. A tall, elegant figure in Liverpool's defence, Gillespie formed a useful partnership with Scottish colleague Alan Hansen. Unfortunately he was always susceptible to injury and seemed no sooner to have returned to the team than he would be back on the treatment table. Had he been less injury-prone he would without question have played many more games and have matured into an outstanding central defender. He played just over 150 league games and liked nothing better than venturing upfield for corners or having a crack at goal. He scored 14 goals for Liverpool. Born in Stirling, he first played for

Falkirk and was capped half a dozen times by Scotland while he was with Liverpool.

GOALS. The most goals Liverpool have ever scored in one game was in their 11–0 victory against Stromgodset in the European Cup Winners' Cup in September 1974. Liverpool also had nine players on the scoresheet that evening – Lindsay, Boersma, Thompson, Heighway, Cormack, Hughes, Smith, Callaghan and Kennedy. Liverpool's highest ever league win was the 9–0 thrashing of Crystal Palace in 1989 at Anfield. Liverpool's highest score in the League Cup was in 1986 when they beat Fulham 10–0.

GOALS – CAREER BEST. The highest goalscorer in the club's history is Ian Rush who between season 1980–81 and the end of season 1994–95 had netted 339 goals for the club.

GOALS – INDIVIDUAL. A number of players have scored five goals in a game for Liverpool. The first was Miller, who netted five in Liverpool's first ever season as they beat Fleetwood 7–0 in December 1892 in a Lancashire League game. A prolific scorer, Miller struck 22 goals in 21 Lancashire League appearances that season. In January 1901 Andy McGuigan became the first Liverpool player to strike five in a Football League match as Liverpool beat Stoke 7–0 at Anfield. It was half a century before the feat was ever repeated, the honour falling to John Evans who netted five as Liverpool beat Bristol Rovers 5–3 at Anfield in September 1954. The only other players to have scored five in one game have been Ian Rush whose goals came against Luton at Anfield in October 1983 as Liverpool won 6–0, and Robbie Fowler who scored all five in the 5–0 win over Fulham in October 1993. There is an instance of a Liverpool player scoring six goals but it was during the war when Liverpool played Southport, so does not officially count. The man who netted six of Liverpool's goals that day was Don Welsh, then a Charlton player guesting with

Liverpool. Welsh subsequently became manager of Liverpool.

GOALS – SEASON. The club's highest league goalscorer in any one season remains Roger Hunt who scored 41 league goals as Liverpool won the second division league title in 1961–62. The highest season's tally for all matches was the 48 goals achieved by Ian Rush in 1983–84. Thirty-two were scored in the league, eight in the Football League Cup, two in the FA Cup and six in Europe.

GOALKEEPERS. For many years Liverpool's telegraphic address at Anfield was 'Goalkeeper' and not without good reason. Over the years the club has boasted some of the finest goalkeepers in the land. Their first outstanding star was the Scottish international Ned Doig who kept goal in the early years of the 20th century. Doig was succeeded by an even more famous name, Sam Hardy, the great England 'keeper who was at Anfield between 1905 and 1912. After Hardy came another international, the Scot Kenny Campbell, who was eventually succeeded by perhaps the finest of them all, the Irishman Elisha Scott who kept goal up to 1934 and was capped 31 times. The South African Arthur Riley then took over until the outbreak of war. After the war Liverpool employed the Welsh international Cyril Sidlow who was eventually followed by the Scottish international Tommy Younger. Since the 1960s Liverpool have had just three regular goalkeepers, all of them outstanding – Tommy Lawrence, Ray Clemence and Bruce Grobbelaar. In 1920 Liverpool set a record by having two of their goalkeepers playing against each other in an international. Kenny Campbell was in goal for Scotland while Elisha Scott was in the Irish line-up.

GODDARD, ARTHUR. Made more than 380 appearances for Liverpool between 1902 and 1914, a startling record for the time. Goddard was born in Stockport and joined Liverpool from Glossop North End, helping them to promotion from the second division in 1905 and the first division title a year later. A fast, skilful winger Goddard was transferred to Cardiff City on the outbreak of war and played with them until 1920. He played for the Football League on three occasions.

GOLDIE, ARCHIE. Born in Ayrshire, Archie Goldie played 130 games for Liverpool between 1895 and 1901. He joined Liverpool from Clyde and helped the Reds to the second division title before joining New Brighton Tower. A strong, resolute defender, Goldie brought some much needed strength to a wilting defence. He was the elder brother of another Liverpool favourite, Bill Goldie.

GOLDIE, BILL. A left-half who made 158 appearances between 1898 and 1904, often playing in front of his elder brother Archie. He came to Liverpool from Clyde and left Anfield for Fulham in 1904 after helping Liverpool to their first ever league championship.

GRACIE, TOM. Centre-forward Tom Gracie made just 32 appearances for Liverpool between 1912 and 1914, scoring five goals. Born in Glasgow, he began his career with Morton before signing for Everton in March 1911. He was transferred to Liverpool along with Billy Lacey in exchange for Harold Uren. He left Liverpool in 1914 and joined Hearts. He played for the Scottish League.

GRAHAM, BOBBY. Had the distinction of scoring a hat trick on his debut as Liverpool beat Aston Villa 5–1 in September 1964. Born in Motherwell, where he had been a member of the same junior side as Ian St John, Graham came to Anfield as an apprentice in November 1960. Over the next 12 years he was to make 96 appearances, scoring 31 goals, but he never quite established himself in the number nine shirt as injuries interrupted his career. He was ever present during the 1969–70 season but the following season made only 13 appearances. Eventually he left to join

Coventry and also had a loan period with Tranmere Rovers before returning home to join Motherwell.

GREAT BRITAIN. Over the years a number of Liverpool amateurs have played soccer for Great Britain. They include Arthur Berry who picked up two Olympic gold medals with the victorious Great Britain side at the 1908 and 1912 games, and Joe Dines who was a gold medal winner in the 1912 Olympics. On a number of occasions there has also been a professional Great Britain side, most notably in 1947 and 1955, when they played The Rest of the World in representative matches. On both occasions Liverpool's Billy Liddell was chosen to play for Great Britain.

GREAT EASTERN. The topmast of the *Great Eastern* ship, one of the first ever iron ships, was erected on the outside corner of the Kop during the early years of the century. The ship had been broken up at Rock Ferry and club officials in search of a flagpole managed to buy it cheaply. The mast was then floated across the Mersey and hauled up Everton Valley by a team of four horses. It still stands in the same spot.

GROBBELAAR, BRUCE. Yet another in a long line of outstanding Anfield goalkeepers. Over the years Grobbelaar has had his critics, most notably when a couple of errors led to the elimination of Liverpool from Europe, but on many an occasion he has also saved Liverpool's skin. Agile and extrovert, the 6ft 1in goalkeeper has never been afraid to race off his goal-line for high clearances or to wander outside his area acting as a sweeper. His antics made him famous but so did his goalkeeping skills, and on his day he was undoubtedly one of the finest in the Football League. Born in 1957 in Durban, South Africa, Grobbelaar spent most of his youth in Zimbabwe where he was also in the army. He joined Liverpool in March 1981 from Vancouver Whitecaps for £250,000 after a period with Crewe Alexan-

Bruce Grobbelaar

dra. He made his debut in August 1981 and was virtually ever present over the next ten years, playing more than 500 games and winning countless medals. A Zimbabwean international, Grobbelaar will always be remembered for his antics during the dramatic penalty shoot-out at the end of the 1984 European Cup final against Roma when his shaking legs act almost certainly distracted a number of penalty-takers. During the summer of 1994 he was transferred to Southampton and was to later face allegations of fixing matches, allegations which he strongly denied.

GUEST PLAYERS. During the Second World War league clubs were allowed to field guest players from local barracks as it was often difficult to obtain leave every week for their own players who might be barracked many miles away. Among those who guested for Liverpool were the Irish international Peter Doherty; the Charlton trio of goalkeeper Sam Bartram, Bert Turner and Don Welsh; the Manchester City and England goalkeeper Frank Swift; England international Stan Cullis and the Everton and England wing-half Cliff Britton.

GUNSON, GORDON. Outside-left of the inter-war years. Gunson spent four years at Anfield making 87 appearances during that time and scoring a useful 26 goals, but it was never enough to bring any silverware to the club. He had arrived in 1930 from Sunderland with glowing reports but injury was to dog his Anfield career. After his Liverpool days were over he was transferred to Swindon Town before returning to his first club, Wrexham.

HALL, BRIAN. University graduate Brian Hall was commonly known as 'Little Bamber' with the other graduate, Steve Heighway, known as 'Big Bamber'. A student of Manchester University, Hall had been given trials with a variety of league clubs but only Liverpool were prepared to take a risk with him. At first it did not look too promising as he lingered in the reserves for three years or so but finally, during the 1970–71 season, he was given his chance. A dynamic little midfielder in the Ian Callaghan mould, Hall beavered away creating space and opportunities for the front-runners. He even managed the occasional goal himself though his contribution was probably never fully appreciated. During his ten years at Anfield he won various honours but was never capped. He left Liverpool in July 1976, having lost his place to the ebullient Jimmy Case, and joined Plymouth Argyle. He later went into teaching but returned to Liverpool as community development officer during the 1990s. He is currently the club's Public Relations Officer.

HANNAH, ANDREW. Right-back signed from crack Scottish club Renton in 1892. It was Hannah's second stint at

Anfield, having already played there with Everton. Hannah helped Liverpool to the second division title in the club's first season in the Football League. As an Everton player Hannah had been a member of the side that won the first division championship in 1891. Hannah was a Scottish international although he never won any further caps while at Liverpool.

HANNAH, DAVID. A possible cousin of Andrew Hannah, they played at Anfield together during the 1890s. He joined Liverpool from Sunderland after a stint with Renton. He later played for Dundee and Woolwich Arsenal. An inside-left, Hannah had won two league championship medals with Sunderland and then picked up a division two champions medal with Liverpool in 1896. He played 31 games, scoring a dozen goals.

HANSEN, ALAN. Alan Hansen's distinguished Anfield career ran almost in tandem with that of Kenny Dalglish. They joined the club within months of each other and left the same week, making over 1,000 appearances between them as well as winning every honour imaginable. Without a doubt Alan Hansen would have to be a contender for any Liverpool all-time great side. He was born in Clackman-nanshire in 1955 and soon took up football with Partick Thistle where he won a division one championship medal. In May 1977 he came to the attention of Liverpool and joined in a £100,000 deal. It took him a while to secure his first team spot but within a short time only injury would deny him his shirt. At first he looked vulnerable but once he had made his usual early mistake his nerves seemed to settle. An elegant defender with the ability to turn quickly, Hansen could outwit most opponents. He won his first Scottish cap in 1979 and went on to receive another 25 caps. But perhaps his greatest international disappointment was to be left out of the 1986 Scottish World Cup squad, a decision which Liverpool supporters found incomprehensible. Playing alongside Mark Lawrenson, Steve Nicol and Phil Neal,

Alan Hansen

Hansen was a member of what was probably the most composed defence the Football League has ever seen. Over the years Hansen became one of the most honoured men in the history of the game with a bundle of European and domestic medals including a phenomenal eight champion-ship medals. When Kenny Dalglish quit Liverpool Hansen was spoken of as a possible successor but rather than allow any speculation to develop he immediately announced his retirement from the game and his intention to develop a career within the media. He had been dogged by injury at various times in his career and during his final season had made few appearances. It was clear that he could not have gone on much longer as a player although there were many who would have liked to have seen him remain at Anfield in some capacity. He totalled 620 appearances for Liverpool.

HANSON, ALF. A useful winger whose football spanned the inter-war years. He came to Anfield in November 1931 and made 166 appearances before joining Chelsea in July 1938. During the war he occasionally guested with Liverpool and most other north-west clubs, including Tranmere, New Brighton, Crewe and Southport. He was capped by England during the war but as a winger never had much chance of full international honours when the likes of Matthews and Finney were around.

HARDY, SAM. Of all the outstanding goalkeepers to have served Liverpool the name of Sam Hardy will always rank among the finest. He joined Liverpool in 1905 from his hometown club of Chesterfield and went on to become the outstanding goalkeeper of his generation. He was spotted by Liverpool manager Tom Watson on the wrong end of a six-goal defeat at Anfield. But Watson had no doubts and quickly signed up the young man. He made his debut in October 1905, taking over from the great Ned Doig, and by the end of the season Liverpool were league champions. Doig had played the first eight games of the season, conceding 20 goals as Liverpool lost five of those matches.

They hardly looked championship contenders yet once Hardy was in position they lost only five more games with Hardy conceding just 26 goals. Hardy's ability was in his positioning and accurate anticipation. He carefully worked out the science of goalkeeping and went on to win 21 England caps, a phenomenal total for those days, in an international career that spanned 13 years. Fourteen of these caps were won while he was at Liverpool. In May 1912 Liverpool surprisingly sold him to Aston Villa where he continued to shine, helping them to two FA Cup final victories. And at the grand old age of 39 Hardy was still playing his part, helping Nottingham Forest to the second division championship in 1922. He died in 1966.

HARKNESS, STEVE. Signed from Carlisle United by Kenny Dalglish when only 20 years old in July 1989. Broke into the first team at the beginning of the 1991–92 season but in later years his opportunities have been limited. A strong, versatile player, Harkness is capable of fitting into the midfield or back four. Capped at England youth level.

HARLEY, JAMES. Full-back who was a member of Liverpool's post-war championship side. A Scot, he came to Liverpool as a 17-year-old in 1934 and remained with them until injury forced his retirement in 1949. One of the fastest defenders in the first division, he had won the famous Powderhall sprint when he was 18 years old – though probably illegally as he was a professional footballer and was forced to use a pseudonym. He won wartime international honours with Scotland.

HARROP, JIM. Centre-half who came to Liverpool in 1907 via Sheffield Wednesday and Rotherham. He stayed at Anfield for five years, winning something of a reputation as a crisp, thoughtful defender. But after 133 games he moved on to Aston Villa where he enjoyed even greater success as a member of their 1913 Cup-winning side. He later played for Sheffield United.

HARROWER, JIMMY. Inside-forward Jimmy Harrower promised much but in the end failed to deliver. A neat inside-forward with considerable skill he had come to Liverpool in an £11,000 move from Hibernian in January 1958. But with Liverpool lingering in the second division it was perhaps not the ideal place for his talents to blossom. He nevertheless won Scottish Under-23 honours. He went north again in the great Shankly clear-out, joining Newcastle United for £15,000, and a year later he was back in Scotland. He made 96 appearances for Liverpool, scoring 21 goals.

HATELEY, TONY. When Tony Hateley arrived from Chelsea for a record fee of £100,000 in June 1967 much was expected. And Hateley, at least to begin with, did not disappoint. In only his third game he struck a hat trick as Liverpool walloped Newcastle 6–0. But the promise was never quite fulfilled. In his first season he struck 27 goals in 52 appearances but then injuries interrupted his career and after just four games the following year he was sold to Coventry for £80,000. The truth was that Liverpool thought they had spotted a potentially better player in Alun Evans, although his career too would be dogged by injury. Yet Hateley on his day had a certain style and dash about him. He was as fine a header of the ball as anyone in the Football League and was fast and direct. With more luck he might well have matured into an outstanding striker but his career was never quite the same after leaving Chelsea and he saw his playing days out among various third and fourth division clubs. His son, the England international Mark Hateley, has probably developed into the player that Tony Hateley might have hoped to become.

HAT TRICK HEROES. Liverpool's hat trick hero has to be Jack Balmer who, during the club's championship season of 1946–47, hit three consecutive hat tricks to become the first player ever to achieve the feat. His first hat trick came in the 3–0 win at Anfield over Portsmouth in November 1946 and included a penalty. The following week he hit four more goals as Liverpool beat Derby 4–1 away. Seven days later at Anfield Arsenal were beaten 4–2 with Balmer scoring three more goals. All ten of his goals were consecutive, with no other Liverpool player scoring in between. Another hat trick hero was Bobby Graham, who hit three goals on his debut against Aston Villa in September 1964 as Liverpool won 5–1. Tony Rowley also hit a hat trick on his debut as Liverpool beat Doncaster 3–2 on the first day of the 1954–55 season.

HEIGHWAY, STEVE. During the 1970s there were few finer sights on the Anfield stage than Steve Heighway galloping down the wing with the ball tightly glued to his boots. He was a greyhound of a winger, sleek, speedy and skilled, with a rare scent for the goalmouth. Although born in Eire he had grown up in England and had studied at Warwick University. He first came to Liverpool's attentions as a member of a highly successful Skelmersdale United side and was recruited, firstly as an amateur, early in 1970. Before long he had turned professional, making his first team debut later that same year. And so, instead of a teaching career, he found himself a professional footballer. He was an exciting player, not afraid to run with the ball and once defenders twigged his style of pushing the ball outside them, he adapted his skills, sliding the ball on to the other foot in order to come inside. He was a vital component in the Liverpool side of the 1970s, winning every conceivable honour with the club. Always a gentleman, he remained a thoughtful and innovative player. Capped 34 times by the Republic of Ireland, he quit Liverpool in 1981 to join the exodus to America where he played for the Minnesota Kicks. He returned to Anfield in the 1980s as Youth Development Officer.

Steve Heighway

HEWITT, JOE. Joe Hewitt was born in Chester but found his way into professional football via Sunderland in 1901. Three years later he arrived at Liverpool and over the next six seasons played more than 150 games, scoring 67 goals.

He was a member of Liverpool's championship-winning side of 1906 when he scored 23 goals. In August 1910 he teamed up with Bolton but returned to Anfield a year later to join the coaching staff, a job he held for many years.

HEYSEL. On the evening of 29 May 1985 at the Heysel stadium in Brussels, so-called Liverpool supporters attacked Juventus fans standing on the terrace at one end of the ground immediately prior to the teams meeting in the European Cup final. Thirty-nine people died as a result. It was one of the blackest and certainly the most shameful episode in the history of Liverpool Football Club.

HICKSON, DAVE. One of the few players to have travelled across Stanley Park from Goodison to Anfield and possibly the only player to have played for all three Merseyside clubs. Tall, blond and bustling, Hickson bore an uncanny resemblance to Roger Hunt but had nowhere near the goalscoring success of his latter-days partner. Hickson was a much travelled player, beginning his career with Ellesmere Port. He joined Everton as a professional in May 1949 and had six successful years at Goodison, although they coincided with a decline in Everton's fortunes. In September 1955 he joined Aston Villa for £17,500 but within two months had deserted them for Huddersfield Town. He rejoined Everton two seasons later and then in November 1959 came to Liverpool in a sensational transfer deal that cost Liverpool £10,500. But Bill Shankly was never really impressed by him even though he managed 37 goals in 60 appearances and in July 1961 he was sold to Cambridge City. He later played for Bury, Tranmere Rovers and Ballymena United before returning to his roots at Ellesmere Port.

HILLSBOROUGH DISASTER. At the start of the FA Cup semi-final between Liverpool and Nottingham Forest at Hillsborough on 15 April 1989, 95 Liverpool supporters died at the Leppings Lane end of the ground. It was the worst sporting tragedy in British history. The disaster led to the Taylor Report and the recommendation that football grounds should be converted to ensure all spectators are seated. A 96th fan died four years later in hospital.

HILLSBOROUGH MEMORIAL. A memorial to those who died in the Hillsborough tragedy was erected alongside the Shankly Gates at Anfield with the names of all the fatalities etched into the stone. An eternal flame burns on the memorial.

HODGSON, DAVID. Centre-forward in the same mould as Dave Hickson. He joined Liverpool in August 1982 from Middlesbrough for £450,000 and although much was expected he proved to be a bitter disappointment. He had plenty of speed and looked to pose a threat but he lacked the luck and instinct of a goalscorer. After just 21 appearances and four goals he was sold for the knockdown price of £125,000 to Sunderland. He later played with Norwich, Sheffield Wednesday and the Spanish club, Jerez. He was capped at England Under-21 level.

HODGSON, GORDON. Unlike his namesake David Hodgson, Gordon Hodgson was to prove one of the finest goalscorers in the club's history. He was a South African, born in Johannesburg, who attracted Liverpool's attention when he played with the visiting South African side in 1925. Liverpool immediately recruited him and over the next 11 seasons he scored 232 goals in 359 games, a remarkable scoring rate even for those days. Fast, sharp and determined, Hodgson set a club record of 36 league goals during the 1930–31 season, yet despite the prolificacy of Hodgson and a cultured half-back line, the 1930s were to prove barren years for Liverpool and at the end of his career all that Hodgson could boast were three England caps. He also played twice for the Football League. Hodgson was a first-class cricketer as well, playing for Lancashire between 1928 and 1933 and also a respected baseball player. In January

1936 he was transferred to Aston Villa and a year later joined Leeds United. After the war he was a member of the coaching staff at Port Vale until his death in 1951.

HOME RECORD. Liverpool's best ever home record was for their first season in league football, 1893–94, when they won all 14 of their second division home games. Liverpool have also had a number of other seasons when they have gone unbeaten at home. They have been 1970–71 (won 11, drew ten), 1976–77 (won 18, drew three), 1978–79 (won 19, drew two), 1979–80 (won 15, drew six), 1987–88 (won 15, drew five).

HOOPER, MIKE. Liverpool second-string goalkeeper for many years with his opportunities limited initially by Bruce Grobbelaar and then by David James. Hooper had arrived at Liverpool as a young graduate from Wrexham in October 1985 but could never quite make the permanent breakthrough into the first team. Yet when he did appear he always performed efficiently and was unlucky to find himself returning to the reserves as soon as Grobbelaar was back to fitness. Joined Newcastle for £550,000.

HOPKIN, FRED. An outside-left of the 1920s with more than 300 games to his credit. Yet despite his many appearances in the Reds' attacks Hopkins managed only nine goals. His first goal coincided remarkably with the outbreak of a fire in the Kemlyn Road Stand. After that it was said that it was a good job he didn't score too often. Hopkin had joined Liverpool from Manchester United where he had already enjoyed a long and distinguished career, though again it was remarkable for its lack of goals. At Anfield he slotted in nicely alongside Harry Chambers and was a useful member of the Liverpool side that won two consecutive titles during the early 1920s.

HOUGHTON, RAY. Ray Houghton was for some time a member of the same Oxford United side as John Aldridge.

Ray Houghton

He was a surprise £850,000 buy in October 1987 and completed Kenny Dalglish's multi-million-pound foray into the transfer market during the summer and autumn of 1987. An attacking, constructive midfielder, Houghton brought a new breadth to the side, providing many an accurate cross for the likes of John Barnes, Peter Beardsley and his old friend John Aldridge. He immediately took over from Craig Johnston and proved to be an outstanding crosser of the ball. He had begun his footballing career with West Ham before joining Fulham and then Oxford United. Despite being a Scot – he was born in Glasgow – he opted to play for the Republic of Ireland, winning more than 50 caps. He helped Liverpool to two league titles and was also a member of two FA cup-winning sides. During the 1991–92 season as Liverpool were dogged with injury Houghton held the side together with his enthusiasm and determination. Unfortunately he did not seem to figure in Graeme Souness' plans, possibly because of the restriction on international players, and he was surprisingly sold to Aston Villa during the summer of 1992 for a little under £1 million. In all he had played more than 150 league games, scoring 28 goals.

HOULDING, JOHN. The founder of Liverpool Football Club. Houlding, a local councillor and brewery owner, was also prominent in the early affairs of Everton Football Club but when Everton left Anfield it also left Houlding behind. Not to be outdone by Everton, Houlding immediately set up a new club and called it Liverpool. Houlding was also a prominent Conservative and Orangeman and was active in the politics of Liverpool City Council for many years. When he died players from both clubs helped carry his coffin at the funeral. He was affectionately known as 'Honest John'.

HOWELL, RABY. It was claimed that the Sheffield-born Raby Howell came from gipsy stock and he was known throughout the game as the gipsy footballer. He began his footballing career as a right-half with Sheffield United and was a member of their championship-winning side of 1898. At the end of that season, however, he joined Liverpool for £200. He had a couple of good seasons at Anfield but unfortunately just as Liverpool found themselves championship contenders in 1901 Howell found himself sidelined and managed just two appearances as the Reds captured their first ever league title. At the end of the season he decided his future lay elsewhere and moved to Preston North End. Howell was capped once while at Liverpool and in all won just two caps for England.

HUGHES, EMLYN. When Bill Shankly signed the 19-year-old half-back from Blackpool for £65,000 in February 1967 he told an astonished press that one day the young man would captain England. Shankly was right and if any player was the epitome of Liverpool during the 1970s it was Emlyn Hughes. Strong, enthusiastic, determined and brave, the Kop nicknamed him 'Crazy Horse'. The son of a rugby league international, Hughes went on to win 59 caps at Anfield to become the most capped England player in the club's history. He won three more caps with Wolves. During his Anfield career Hughes also picked up two European Cup winners' medals, two UEFA Cup medals, four league championship medals and an FA Cup winners' medal. With his Liverpool career clearly drawing to a close he was transferred for £90,000 to Wolverhampton Wanderers in August 1979. He went on to help them win the Football League Cup, the one trophy that had eluded him at Liverpool. Hughes remained with Liverpool for 13 seasons, making 657 appearances and scoring 48 goals and was undoubtedly one of the toughest half-backs in the club's history.

HUGHES, LAURIE. Liverpool-born Laurie Hughes began his footballing career with Tranmere Rovers as an amateur before signing professional forms with Liverpool in 1943. In his first league season, after the war, he helped Liverpool

Emlyn Hughes

to the league title and went on to play for the club for another 11 years. A tall, strong centre-half, he was a member of the 1950 Cup final side and was also picked for England's abortive trip to the 1950 World Cup finals. He played three times during the finals, including the ill-fated game against the USA. They were to be his last games for England. In all he made more than 300 appearances for Liverpool, scoring just one goal, though serious injury meant that he missed the best part of two whole seasons. He retired in May 1960.

HUNDRED GOALS. Liverpool have only once scored more than one hundred league goals in a season and that was in 1895–96 when they struck 106 goals as they won the second division championship. In the 1961–62 season, again as they won the second division title, they came within one goal of hitting a century of league goals.

HUNDRED THOUSAND. Liverpool's first £100,000 player was Tony Hateley, signed from Chelsea for exactly that sum in June 1967.

HUNT, ROGER. One of the most prolific goalscorers of the 1960s, Roger Hunt for many years held Liverpool's record for the number of goals scored for the club as well as the highest goal tally for a season. He came to Liverpool as a youth in 1958 and remained with the club for 11 years, during which time he struck 285 league goals. He made his first appearance in a red shirt in September 1959 and went on to make 489 appearances. He hit more than 20 league goals in a season on seven occasions, his best during the 1961–62 season as he netted 41 league goals to create a new club record and help Liverpool to the second division title. Some reckoned he would find life in the first division more difficult but, on the contrary, Hunt warmed to his task and although he never scored anywhere near as many goals in a season his contribution was still impressive. He formed as effective a goalscoring partnership with Ian St John as any

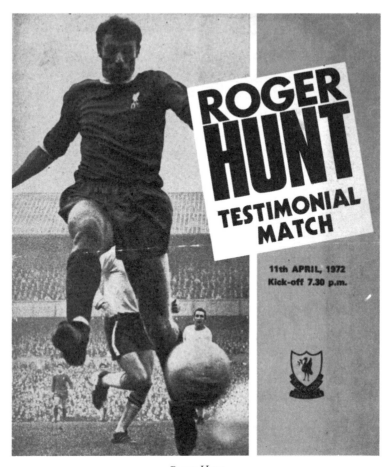

Roger Hunt

the club had ever known then or even since. With his sweeping blond hair and speed Hunt always seemed to be in the right place at the right time. But he had his critics, particularly those who followed the fortunes of England, who reckoned he was never worth his international place, particularly with Jimmy Greaves around. But Alf Ramsey remained an admirer of his poaching instincts and rewarded him with 34 caps. And during the 1966 World Cup finals Ramsey's decision to play Hunt instead of Greaves was to prove crucial to England's fortunes. The Kop dubbed him

'Sir Roger Hunt'. He left Liverpool in December 1969, joining Bolton Wanderers for £31,000, and retired in 1972 to work in the family haulage business.

HUTCHISON, DON. Signed from Hartlepool United by manager Kenny Dalglish for £175,000 in November 1990, Gateshead-born Hutchison did not break through into the first team until the 1992–93 season when Graeme Souness gave him his chance. He made his debut in the 4–0 defeat of Notts County on 31 March 1992. A tall, 6ft 1in, midfielder, Hutchison liked to power his way into the penalty area to snap up any loose goalscoring chances and looked set for a long and dazzling Anfield career. Sold by Roy Evans to West Ham United during the 1994–95 season.

HYSEN, GLENN. The stylish Swedish international was something of a surprise signing from Italian club Fiorentina during the summer of 1989. Hysen had been expected to join Manchester United but with United quibbling over the price, Dalglish smartly jumped in and had him signed up before United or anyone else had the time to respond. Hysen's first season in the Liverpool defence turned out to be his best. He was cool, authoritative and experienced and played a major part in Liverpool's drive to the title. After that the years seemed to catch up with him. The following season he looked more vulnerable and was caught out on a number of occasions. For a brief spell he even captained the club but the arrival of Graeme Souness brought an awkward end to his career and in 1992 he returned home to Sweden. Hysen's football career began with third division Swedish side Vwarta until he was transferred to Gothenburg in 1978 for a fee of £2,500. In 1982 he was a member of the Gothenburg side that won the UEFA Cup, and within a season had been snapped up by Dutch club PSV Eindhoven. After three seasons in Holland Hysen returned to Sweden, rejoining Gothenburg, who promptly went on to win the UEFA Cup again. And that was enough for Fiorentina to step in with a £700,000 bid that took him to Italy.

I

INTER-CLUB TRANSFERS. Interest has traditionally focused on how many players have moved across Stanley Park. In the past only a handful of players have made the short journey but in recent years the number has been bumped up by the transfers of Peter Beardsley, Gary Ablett, Kevin Sheedy and David Johnson. Others who made the trek over the years include Dave Hickson, Fred Geary, Bill Lacey, Harold Uren and Tom Gracie. Perhaps the most interesting inter-club transfer these days is the lack of deals between Liverpool and Manchester United. Since the war only one player, Phil Chisnall, has made the journey along the M62 when he came to Liverpool from United in April 1964.

INTER-LEAGUE MATCHES. There have been six inter-league matches played at Anfield with the Football League playing the Irish League in all six games, winning all bar one. The first game was played in October 1911 when the Football League won 4–0. The last game was in 1959 when 30,000 saw the Football League win 5–2. Liverpool's Johnny Wheeler and Alan A'Court played for the Football League that day.

INTER MILAN. The crack Italian club were Liverpool's opponents in the semi-final of the European Cup in 1965. Liverpool won the first leg 3–1 in a game played just days after they had won the FA Cup. In the second leg, however, Liverpool went down 3–0 in front of 90,000 in the San Siro stadium, losing the tie 3–4 on aggregate. Much was made of some dubious refereeing decisions in that second leg with Bill Shankly and many others convinced that the referee had been fixed.

INTERNATIONAL CAPS – FIRST. The first Liverpool player ever to be capped was the winger Harry Bradshaw who played for England against Ireland in February 1897. England won 6–0.

INTERNATIONAL CAPS – MOST. Liverpool's most capped player is Emlyn Hughes, who represented England 59 times while he was at Anfield.

INTERNATIONAL MATCHES. Anfield has been host to only a handful of international matches. Perhaps the most memorable was the World Cup clash between Scotland and Wales in October 1977. The game, a decider for the World Cup finals, was won 2–0 by Scotland and was watched by a crowd of 50,000 who paid record receipts of over £150,000. Liverpool had three players on duty that night – Joey Jones and John Toshack for Wales, and Kenny Dalglish who scored Scotland's second goal. Five other internationals have also been played at Anfield. The first was in 1889 when England beat Ireland 6–1. England have also played Wales at Anfield on three occasions, in 1905, 1922 and 1931, winning all three games. In 1926 Ireland forced a memorable draw against England, and during the Second World War England and Wales drew 2–2 in front of a crowd of 38,000. In 1963 the England Under-23 side beat West Germany and in 1981 the England Under-21 side defeated Eire by a single goal. In December 1994 England B faced Ireland B at Anfield with England winning 2–0.

IRVINE, ALAN. A strong attacker who had the misfortune to be playing at Anfield when there was a proliferation of outstanding forwards. He had joined the club from Falkirk in 1986 for £75,000. Sadly, he made just two appearances, both as substitute, and in 1987 moved back to Scotland, joining Dundee United for £100,000.

IRWIN, COLIN. Liverpool-born defender who elsewhere might have had a distinguished career. But at Anfield his appearances were limited to just 26 games. He was nevertheless a useful player to have in reserve and managed three goals in his few outings. He was transferred to Swansea in August 1981 for £350,000 and later became their club captain before injury forced early retirement.

J

JACKSON, BRIAN. When Brian Jackson arrived as an 18-year-old at Anfield in 1951 he came with glowing reports. Born in Walton-on-Thames, he had turned professional with Leyton Orient, making his debut when he was only 17 years old. He was transferred to Liverpool for £6,500 plus the Reds winger Donald Woan. Unfortunately he joined a Liverpool side that was in decline and although he made a bright start to his Anfield career he never really prospered. Perhaps too much was expected of him and he was probably given too heavy a responsibility too early. Yet over the next seven years he went on to play 124 games, mainly at outside-right, and netted 12 goals before he was sold to Port Vale in 1958. He later had a successful spell at Peterborough.

JACKSON, THE REVEREND JIMMY. Football has attracted a few misfits in its time but Jimmy Jackson must go down as one of the oddest. A deeply religious man, Jackson studied for the church while he was at Anfield, attending Liverpool University and later Cambridge University. Born in Newcastle in 1900, he joined Liverpool from Aberdeen in 1925 and finally quit the game when he was ordained as a minister in 1933. Ostensibly a full-back, Jackson made 224 appearances for the club but could play just about anywhere. Moreover, he may have been a sensitive and religious man away from football but on the field he was as tough as they come. Jackson was never capped but he did play for the Football League against the Irish League at Bloomfield Road in 1931. Jackson came from a famous sporting family. His father played for Rangers, Newcastle and Arsenal, while his brother played for Tranmere. He also had a cousin who played Test cricket for Australia.

JAMES, DAVID. Young goalkeeper signed from Watford for £1 million during the summer of 1992. In his first season at Anfield he was plunged straight into the first team but it was not a happy experience. A weakened Liverpool defence gave him little cover and the goals began to pour past him. Although few of them were his fault it was enough to shake his confidence and part way through the season he gave way to Mike Hooper and then Bruce Grobbelaar. He eventually returned in February 1993 for a Liverpool win at Highbury, James's first clean sheet as a Liverpool player. A big, strong goalkeeper, James is one of the tallest men ever to play for Liverpool. Following the resignation of Graeme Souness, James became the number one choice and was an ever-present throughout the 1994–95 season. Has won England B honours and a winner's medal in the Coca-Cola Cup.

JOHNSON, DAVID. One of the few players to have made the short journey both ways across Stanley Park. Johnson came to Liverpool from Ipswich for a record £200,000 in August 1976. A Liverpool lad, he had begun his playing days with Everton where he showed early promise. In October 1971, however, he was transferred to Ipswich where he began to mature into a useful centre-forward, winning three England caps. He was eventually tempted to Liverpool but initially failed to make the grade and was exiled to the reserves for a time. During his first couple of

David Johnson

seasons his outings were few and far between and with the arrival of Kenny Dalglish it seemed that Liverpool were about to discard him. But he decided to stay and went on to prove his worth, forming an effective partnership with Dalglish that led to more England honours and a few trophies for Liverpool. He won a European Cup winners' medal in 1981 plus three league championship medals. A modern type of centre-forward, slim, sharp and a neat passer of the ball, Johnson was an integral part of a fine Liverpool side. The 1981–82 season, however, saw the emergence of Ian Rush and Johnson's outings were limited from that moment on. At the end of the season he decided to return to his former club Everton, who paid £100,000 for his services. But he never quite hit it off at Goodison and subsequently went to Manchester City before joining Tulsa Roughnecks in the United States. He made 128 appearances for Liverpool, scoring 55 goals.

JOHNSON, DICK. Began his footballing career in his native north-east, guesting during the First World War with Sunderland. He came to Liverpool in January 1920 but made only one appearance that season. The following season he scored 13 times in 26 league appearances in a Liverpool side that was clearly edging towards honours. The following season they won the league title but Johnson missed the entire season with a knee injury. However, he returned the next year, scoring 14 league goals as Liverpool captured a second successive championship. But the knee injury persisted and over the next two years he played only 14 games. Said to be a fast and lively centre-forward, he was eventually transferred to Stoke in 1925 and helped them to the third division north title. He later played with New Brighton and died at the age of 38.

JOHNSON, THOMAS (TOSH). Was something of a scoring sensation with his first club, Manchester City, hitting 38 goals in 39 league outings, still a record for the Maine Road club. He enjoyed ten highly successful seasons

101

with City before he was surprisingly transferred to Everton. The anger of City fans at his leaving was only compounded when Johnson helped Everton beat City in the 1933 FA Cup final. He also picked up first and second division championship medals with Everton as well as three more England caps to add to the two he had already won. When he was transferred to Liverpool in March 1934 he was 34 years of age and clearly past his best. He played just 37 times for the Reds, scoring eight goals before he was transferred to Darwen two years later.

JOHNSTON, CRAIG. Born in South Africa, Johnston spent his early days in Australia where he played for Lake McQuarrie and Sydney City. After seeing Middlesbrough play in Australia he decided to try his luck in England and went immediately to Middlesbrough for a trial. He was initially unsuccessful but tried again the following year and was finally taken on by the north-east club. He made his league debut in 1978 and although he had only four more appearances over the next 18 months he became a regular choice during the 1979-80 season. In April 1981 he followed Graeme Souness to Anfield in a £580,000 deal. Unmistakable with his long bushy hair, Johnston was a lively midfielder who usually operated down the flanks where he was always willing to take on defenders. His efforts were often wasted by his poor crosses but he nevertheless was an integral part of a Liverpool side that dominated English football throughout the 1980s. He could also score goals, none more important than the one that put Liverpool ahead in the 1986 Cup final against Everton. He won a European Cup winners' medal in 1984 plus five championship medals as well as an FA Cup winners' medal. He even played for the England Under-21 side. Joe Fagan did not always take to Johnston's maverick attitude and for a time he was out of favour. However, the appointment of Dalglish as manager brought a new, though brief, lease of life. A serious accident to his sister led to his eventual retirement and Johnston returned home to Australia at the end of the 1987–88 season to look after her and to pursue his other interest, photography.

JONES, BILL. Grandfather of the current Liverpool full-back Rob Jones, Bill Jones came to Anfield a year before the Second World War broke out. During the war he won the Military Medal and did not make his league debut until 1946 when he made 26 appearances in Liverpool's championship side. Though usually to be found at full-back, he could play just about anywhere, enjoying himself as much at centre-half as at centre-forward. He even played at centre-half for England, making two appearances against Portugal and Belgium. He also played for the Football League against the Irish League. Jones enjoyed eight seasons at Anfield, making 278 appearances and scoring 17 goals. He also appeared in the 1950 Cup final against Arsenal at left-half. In May 1954 he quit Liverpool to become player-manager at Ellesmere Port but returned to Anfield as a scout during the 1960s and 1970s.

JONES, JOEY. Few players can have demonstrated the never-say-die spirit of Liverpool Football Club as much as Joey Jones. Always popular with the fans, Jones played his heart out for his club and country. He joined Liverpool from Wrexham in July 1975 and went on to play 97 games, usually as a left full-back. Strong and quick, Jones was as tough a full-back as any in the first division. He gave outstanding service and many felt that he left Anfield prematurely when he returned to Wrexham in September 1978. He had played only three seasons, although it sometimes seemed he had been there a lifetime. He later played with Chelsea and Huddersfield. He won numerous medals at Anfield plus 18 Welsh caps and went on to win a total of 72 caps.

JONES, LEE. A Graeme Souness signing for Liverpool from Wrexham. Now a Welsh Under-21 international although has made only a handful of appearances for the Reds. Played just 39 games for Wrexham scoring 10 goals before joining Liverpool.

JONES, ROB. Signed by Graeme Souness from Crewe in 1991 for £300,000, Jones showed his worth on his debut against Manchester United at Old Trafford where a weakened Liverpool side battled bravely for a draw with Jones the star of the proceedings. Within four months he had won his first England cap, playing against France at Wembley, as he continued to give a series of quality performances that promised much for one so young. He won a Cup winners' medal with Liverpool in his first season but injury brought a temporary halt to his blossoming career the following season. After recovering from injury his career carried on where it had left off. Further international honours have come his way as well as a winner's medal from the Coca-Cola Cup.

JUVENTUS. Liverpool have played the famous Italian club on three occasions in European competition. They first met in September 1966 in Liverpool's first ever game in the Cup Winners' Cup with Liverpool losing the first leg 1–0 but winning the second leg at Anfield 2–0 to qualify for the next round. The clubs' next meeting was in a one-off game to decide the European Super Cup in 1985 and on a snowbound pitch in Turin Juventus won 2–0. Four months later they faced each other again, this time in the final of the European Cup at the Heysel stadium. Juventus won 1–0 that night but the game was overshadowed by events off the field. Since that tragedy the two clubs and the two cities have formed a strong bond of friendship.

K

KAY, GEORGE. Liverpool manager between 1936 and 1951. Born in Manchester, he began his footballing career with Bolton Wanderers but made only three appearances for the Lancashire club during the early part of the 1910–11 season. After a row with Bolton, Kay tried his luck across the Irish Sea with the famous Belfast Celtic and became the first Englishman ever to skipper an Irish league club. During the First World War he served with the Royal Garrison Artillery and when hostilities ceased returned to league soccer with West Ham United, making his debut in September 1919. Over the next seven seasons centre-half Kay became the first West Ham player to make more than 200 appearances for the club and even captained the side in the famous Cup final of 1923, played at Wembley for the first time, when West Ham met his old club Bolton. Unfortunately Kay was not destined to become the first man to lift the trophy at Wembley as West Ham went down 2–0. Kay finally retired in 1926 and was invited to take charge at Luton where he ruled for a couple of seasons before Southampton appointed him as their manager in 1931. He was particularly successful at the Dell, keeping the under-resourced club in the second division, but soon came to the attention of Liverpool, desperately searching for a new manager following the resignation of George Patterson through ill health. In May 1936 Liverpool appointed Kay as their manager and he was to remain at the helm through the war years until 1951. Kay's finest deal during the pre-war years was almost certainly the signing of Billy Liddell which in the first season after the war paid handsome dividends as Liddell and one of his other signings Albert Stubbins led the Reds to the league championship. It was to be Kay's greatest triumph. At the time he also introduced some other fine players to Anfield including Laurie Hughes, Bob Paisley, Eddie Spicer and Ray Lambert. Three years after their league championship success Liverpool also reached the Cup final but were beaten 2–0 by Arsenal. It was to be Kay's last success. He was already a sick man and within a year had decided to retire. He died in April 1965.

KEMLYN ROAD STAND. The Kemlyn Road was originally a banking of terraces but after Liverpool had won their second championship in 1906 the directors decided to construct a stand on the banking. At the same time they also sanctioned work on a huge banking at one end of the ground which later became known as the Kop. The stand on the Kemlyn Road was a barrel-roofed one, just like the Main Stand and the one at the Anfield Road end of the ground. In front of the new stand was an uncovered paddock and later a Boys' Pen. In 1963 the old Kemlyn Road Stand was pulled down and in its place a cantilevered stand was erected at the then enormous cost of £350,000. It was an all-seated stand with room for 6,700 spectators and was opened on 22 August 1964. At the end of the 1991–92 season work began on extending the old stand by constructing a tier on top with executive boxes, suites, and offices, providing seating for a total of 11,400 spectators. It has now been renamed the Centenary Stand.

KEMP, DIRK. South African-born goalkeeper who played

for Liverpool between 1936 and 1944. Kemp was one of several South Africans to join Liverpool and is one of four Springboks to have kept goal for the club. He made his debut in March 1937, just three months after arriving in England, and went on to make 30 league appearances. He also played wartime football with Southport, York and Brighton.

KENNEDY, ALAN. Sunderland-born Alan Kennedy had played for Newcastle against Liverpool in the 1974 Cup final. Four years later he joined Liverpool for £330,000 and was to prove one of Bob Paisley's canniest buys. Kennedy was in the traditional mould of full-backs, tough and hard-tackling, but had added a further element to the usual repertoire with his instinctive runs upfield that resulted in many a vital goal. His most memorable goals were to come in the European Cup finals of 1981 and 1984. Against Real Madrid in Paris it was Kennedy cutting into the penalty area before firing in a wicked shot from the narrowest of angles that brought the only goal of the game. Three years later he was a matchwinner again with a perfectly executed penalty against Roma in the European Cup final. In practice the day before he had missed every penalty attempt but in the Olympic Stadium with 70,000 breathing down his neck he stepped up and coolly fired the most important penalty kick in the club's history high into the back of the net. Kennedy, or 'Barney' as the fans called him, was a great favourite with the Kop. He went on to make 247 appearances for Liverpool, scoring 15 goals before he was transferred to his native Sunderland in September 1985 for £100,000. Kennedy won five league championship medals as well as his European honours. He was also capped by England twice.

KENNEDY, MARK. Signed by Liverpool late in the 1994–95 season from Millwall for £1 million, making him the most expensive 18-year-old in football history. It is a fee that could also rise to as much as £2 million depending upon his progress. At Millwall he had scored a spectacular goal against Arsenal and had won rave notices for some of his performances. Operates on the left midfield and with his pace and ability can take the ball to the bye line. He is also a fine crosser of the ball. He enjoyed a few games in the Liverpool first team towards the end of the season, showing considerable promise. Born in Dublin, he played just over 50 games for Millwall before Roy Evans stepped in with his record bid. Irish Under-21 international.

KENNEDY, RAY. Bill Shankly's parting gesture when he quit during the summer of 1974 was to sign the Arsenal centre-forward Ray Kennedy. Kennedy had been a key member of the Gunners' side that clinched the Double in 1971 though the £180,000 arrival of Kennedy was somewhat overshadowed by Shankly's resignation. Kennedy began his Anfield career as a striker, playing a similar role to the one he had at Highbury. Unfortunately he was something of a disappointment and scored only five goals in 23 outings in his first season. The following season he was little better and was sent to the reserves to learn the Liverpool way. It could well have marked the end of Kennedy's Anfield career but Bob Paisley, in a master stroke, decided instead to convert him into a midfielder. Kennedy was to prove a revelation. From then on he was an ever present and became one of the most effective midfielders in the first division. He was strong and powerful, could win the ball and hold it comfortably and liked nothing better than sneaking into the area to lap up any opportunities or hovering just outside the box ready to fire any loose chances back at goal. Kennedy went on to win countless honours at Anfield, plus 17 England caps, adding European medals to the domestic ones he had already won with Arsenal. He was to be one of the most honoured men in the game and was capped by England on 17 occasions, scoring three goals. In January 1982 he was transferred to Swansea for £160,000 before returning to his native northeast. It was later discovered that Kennedy had Parkinson's

Ray Kennedy

Disease and a special match was staged between Liverpool and Arsenal to help him finance medical treatment. It was always said that when Kennedy was on song, so too were Liverpool. It is impossible to overstate the value of Kennedy to Liverpool during the outstanding years of the 1970s.

KEEGAN, KEVIN. On a pound-for-pound basis Kevin Keegan has to go down as one of the best buys in the club's history. He was certainly Bill Shankly's finest signing. Keegan was born in Doncaster and kicked off his playing career with fourth division Scunthorpe United in December 1968. Eighteen months later, and with only a handful of games behind him, Liverpool snapped him up for a mere £35,000. Six years later they sold him for £500,000. In between he had inspired Liverpool to the European Cup, two UEFA Cups, the FA Cup and three league titles. He had also been voted Footballer of the Year and had collected 29 England caps, even captaining his country. Keegan was a superstar, articulate and forthcoming, as well as being one of the finest players to ever wear a Liverpool shirt. He may have been slightly on the short side but could rise as high as any tall striker, flicking the ball down to one of his colleagues, usually John Toshack. He was also a difficult man to shake off the ball and when he tumbled he seemed to bounce straight up again. He set up a formidable goalscoring partnership with Toshack and in 321 games for Liverpool he netted 100 goals. Keegan had just about everything. He could carry the ball, he had pace, he could head the ball and had a crisp, accurate shot. He could also defend and was usually the first attacker back into defence. He set a fine example to other players and for the club. But his departure from Liverpool was to be tinged with bitterness, not on the part of Keegan but more on the part of the fans. Keegan was the first player to leave Anfield for foreign shores and although he was as firm a favourite of the Kop as anyone, his departure was not greeted with universal enthusiasm. There was an accusation of disloyalty that he

Kevin Keegan

The Kop

should leave the side when he was at his best. But Keegan wanted to widen his experience and had already given Liverpool an extra season when club officials had agreed a deal with Real Madrid. He finally left in the summer of 1977, his last game being the European Cup final against Borussia Moenchengladbach, and went off to join Hamburg. He was equally successful in West Germany, helping Hamburg to the Bundesliga title and to the European Cup final. He was also named European Footballer of the Year. He later returned to England, having spells with Southampton and Newcastle. He became manager of Newcastle United in 1992, taking them into the Premier League by the end of the following season.

KOP. The most famous terracing in football. It was built in 1906 as a reward to the fans following Liverpool's second championship victory. Over the years it changed little and was until 1994 still a large terracing behind the goal at Anfield which at its height could hold 27,000 spectators. It was named after a famous battle during the Boer War which took place at Spion Kop on 24 January 1900. More than 300 men lost their lives during the battle, most of them from the Lancashire Fusiliers and many of them from Liverpool and south Lancashire. The name Spion Kop was suggested by Ernest Edwards, then the sports editor of the Liverpool Daily Post and Echo. The Kop was at first open to the elements but in 1928 it was slightly extended and roofed. The new roofed Kop was formally opened by John McKenna, then the President of the Football League, on the first day of the 1928–29 season. The Kop then remained much the same although the capacity was lowered to comply with various legislation. By 1993 the maximum capacity was down to 16,480. Its length was 394 feet, its width from top to bottom is 135 feet and its height at the back is 50 feet. In all there were exactly 100 steps on its terracing. At the end of the 1993–94 season the Kop was demolished to comply with the recommendations of the Taylor Report and in its place a new all-seater stand was erected with a capacity of

13,000. During the 1960s the Kop became even more famous when its inhabitants began to sing and chant. Its fame subsequently spread throughout the world as football fans everywhere took up the chants and songs that had originated on the Kop.

KOZMA, ISTVAN. Hungarian midfielder signed from Dunfermline for £300,000 during 1992 but made only a few appearances in the Liverpool first team before he returned to Hungary in the summer of 1993.

L

LACEY, BILLY. Irrepressible little Irish international signed from Everton in February 1912. Lacey was part of an exchange deal that took Tom Gracie and Harry Uren to Goodison. Liverpool got the better of the move with Lacey going on to make 257 appearances for the Reds as well as adding to his collection of Irish caps while Uren and Gracie only managed 37 appearances between them for the Blues. A versatile player, Lacey was equally at home on the wing or as a half-back. His career really took off at Anfield and he was a member of the FA Cup final side that lost to Burnley in 1914. He was also a regular member of Liverpool's two league championship sides of the early 1920s. Born in Wexford, he had begun his playing days with Shelbourne before joining Everton in 1908. He left Liverpool in 1924 and ended his career with New Brighton. He was capped 23 times by Ireland, winning ten of those during his time at Goodison Park and the other 13 while at Anfield.

LAMBERT, RAY. Welsh defender who had the distinction of being the youngest ever player to be signed by a league club when he joined Liverpool as an amateur at the age of 13 years and 189 days. That was before the Second World War but it was not until after the war that Lambert finally made his debut. He was a regular member of the league championship side of 1946–47 and also appeared in the 1950 FA Cup final. Equally at home either as a right-back or a left-back, Lambert was a strong, no-nonsense tackler and was an outstanding servant to the club, making over 300 appearances. During the war he guested with New Brighton and Reading. He retired in 1956 and was capped five times by Wales.

LANE, FRANK. Wallasey-born goalkeeper Frank Lane began his league career with Tranmere Rovers, making 76 league appearances with the Birkenhead club before joining Liverpool as understudy to Ray Clemence. Unfortunately Clemence's consistency and fitness restricted Lane's full team appearances to just one game. He finally left Liverpool in July 1975, joining Notts County, but again found himself playing second fiddle to another fine goalkeeper and made just two appearances for the second division club.

LATHOM, GEORGE. Holder of the Military Cross and the rank of captain in the Royal Welsh Fusiliers, Lathom served in the Boer War as well as the First World War. He made just 18 appearances for Liverpool, joining them in 1902. Seven years later he left, signing up with Southport Central. He subsequently became trainer of Cardiff City, taking them to two FA Cup finals, and also managed the Welsh national side. He was capped ten times by Wales.

LAWLER, CHRIS. One of the most distinguished defenders in the history of Liverpool Football Club. He was known in Anfield circles as 'the Silent Knight' for his quiet, unassuming ways but dependable and sturdy defending. Lawler joined Liverpool directly from school and turned professional in October 1960. He made his debut two years later and went on to make more than 500 appearances in a red shirt, picking up league championship, FA Cup and

Chris Lawler

UEFA Cup winning medals over the next 16 years. He even managed a respectable 61 goals for the club, scoring 11 of those in 66 European appearances. Lawler's forays upfield in European competition seemed to take continental defences by surprise and on more than one occasion proved the difference between Liverpool and their opponents. Lawler left Anfield in 1975 to join up with his old team-mate Ian St John, then managing Portsmouth. He later played with Stockport County and coached in Norway and at Wigan Athletic before Joe Fagan recruited him as reserve team trainer at Anfield. A year after Kenny Dalglish's appointment as manager, however, Lawler was fired and he retired gracefully to North Wales to help run his business. He was capped four times by England, though many argued that he deserved far more honours than that.

LAWRENCE, TOMMY. Liverpool goalkeeper of the 1960s,

affectionately known by Kopites as 'the Flying Pig'. When Bill Shankly arrived at Anfield in 1959 Lawrence was lingering in the reserves. Shankly soon promoted him and the Scotsman went on to make almost 400 appearances for the club. Born in Ayrshire, Lawrence had come to Anfield via Warrington in 1957. He was never a spectacular goalkeeper but was always dependable. What he lacked in height he made up for with his acute positional sense and he also had an athleticism that defied his bulk. Defenders liked him; they knew where they were and could trust in his reliability. He was capped three times by Scotland, although his international appearances were never happy events and he often found himself unfairly blamed for some of the goals. The arrival of Ray Clemence spelled an inevitable end to Lawrence's Anfield career and in September 1971 he signed for Tranmere Rovers where he made a further 80 appearances before bowing out of the professional game.

LAWRENSON, MARK. Without a doubt Mark Lawrenson was one of the finest defenders the modern game has ever seen and his early retirement left Liverpool mourning his loss for many seasons. With Steve Nicol, Alan Hansen and Phil Neal alongside him, it was probably the safest back four British football has ever seen. Lawrenson was a surprise buy from Brighton. He had made few headlines and there was little hint of what was to come even though manager Bob Paisley unhesitatingly paid out a record fee of £900,000 for him. Born in Preston, Lawrenson had begun his days at Deepdale before joining Brighton in 1977. He came to Anfield during the summer of 1981 and quickly slotted into the defence. Tall, fast, and one of the surest tacklers in the game, there were few attackers who ever got the better of him. In 1984 he picked up a European Cup winners' medal and during his years at Anfield also won four league championship medals, an FA Cup winners' medal and three League Cup medals. Although he had been born in Lancashire, Lawrenson opted to play for the Republic of Ireland, a decision which English football was

119

Mark Lawrenson

to deeply regret. He went on to make 37 appearances for Eire. In 1986 injuries began to affect his career. He had to pull out of the 1985 European Cup final with a shoulder injury after just minutes and then the following season sustained an Achilles tendon injury which eventually led to his premature retirement. It was a grave loss to Liverpool and in April 1988 he took up the offer of a managerial post at Oxford United. After some success, however, he was sacked by the club's owners, the Maxwells, when he questioned the sale of Dean Saunders, a deal done without his knowledge. The subsequent success of Saunders and the demise of the Maxwells reflected well on Lawrenson, who is still involved in football as an agent and a broadcaster.

LEAGUE CHAMPIONSHIP HAT TRICK. Liverpool won three successive league titles between 1981 and 1984 to equal the pre-war achievements of Hudderfield Town and Arsenal.

LEAGUE CUP. See **FOOTBALL LEAGUE CUP.**

LEAGUE GOALS – CAREER HIGHEST. Roger Hunt holds the Anfield record for the most league goals with a career total of 245 goals between 1980 and 1992.

LEAGUE GOALS – LEAST CONCEDED. During the 1978–79 season Liverpool conceded just 16 goals in 42 games, a record for the Football League. Only four of those goals were conceded at Anfield.

LEAGUE GOALS – MOST INDIVIDUAL. Roger Hunt holds the Liverpool record for the most league goals in a season with 41 scored in the second division during the 1961–62 season.

LEAGUE GOALS – MOST SCORED. Liverpool's highest goal tally in the Football League was during the 1895–96 season when they scored 106 goals to win the second division championship.

LEAGUE POINTS – HIGHEST. Liverpool hold the record for the highest number of points in a season in the first division, with 68 during the 1978–79 season to establish a new record under the old two points system. Under the three points for a win system their highest tally is 90, achieved during the 1987–88 season. This is also a record for the first division, equal with Everton, though Liverpool played two games less.

LEAGUE VICTORY – HIGHEST. 10–1 versus Rotherham in division two, 18 February 1896.

LEE, SAMMY. Liverpool-born Sammy Lee came to Anfield as a 16-year-old in 1975 and made his debut in April 1978, even scoring, against Leicester City. Always popular with the fans, Lee was a busy midfielder, devoted to Liverpool and as passionate about the club as any player who has ever worn a red shirt. At 5ft 7in and weighing in at just over ten stones, Lee did not at first appear to have the build of a footballer. But it was a deception: he was as fast, resilient and determined as any man on the pitch. He was a driving force, urging the team forward all the time with his boyish enthusiasm but just as ready to sprint back into defence. It took him a couple of seasons to establish himself but by mid-1980 he was first choice and went on to win a crop of honours, including two European Cup winners' medals, three league championship medals and four League Cup medals. He also won 14 England caps and scored twice for his country. But with the 1984–85 season came a loss of form and although he survived a further year or so, his appearances were restricted. In August 1986 he was transferred to Queen's Park Rangers for £200,000. A year later he went to Spain, joining Osasuna. But like so many Liverpudlians he found his way back to the city, and when Phil Thompson was sacked by manager Graeme Souness, Lee was appointed in his place as reserve team trainer. In all

Sammy Lee

he made more than 270 appearances for Liverpool, scoring 19 goals.

LEISHMAN, TOMMY. Tommy Leishman arrived at Anfield from St Mirren for £9,000 in the autumn of 1959, shortly before Bill Shankly's arrival at the club. He was still only in his early 20s and much was expected of him. A craggy, left-sided midfielder, he possessed a useful turn of speed and was a tough tackler but hardly a quality passer of

123

the ball. In the end he was a frustrating sort of player, the kind who could race into open spaces but then fail to deliver the telling pass or shot at goal. Shankly persevered with him while Liverpool struggled to escape the second division and in their second division championship season he missed just one game. But the following season in the higher division his lack of quality was all too apparent and Willie Stevenson's arrival marked the end of his Anfield career. So he returned north, joining Hibernian for £10,000. In all he played 119 games in a red shirt, scoring seven goals.

LEWIS, HENRY. Birkenhead-born inside-forward of the inter-war years. Lewis joined Liverpool from local football in 1916. Playing in wartime soccer he made 99 appearances for the Reds, netting an impressive 56 goals. But once league football kicked off again he was never a regular although he did manage 19 games as Liverpool clinched the league title during the 1921–22 season. His solitary goal that season, however, was far from impressive form and before long he was on his way, joining Hull City in October 1923.

LEWIS, KEVIN. Although he was born on Merseyside, Kevin Lewis's career kicked off in Yorkshire with Sheffield United. He came to Liverpool in June 1960 for a club record fee of £13,000. But it was a deal that only worked out briefly. In his first season he netted 19 league goals in just 32 appearances and then struck ten in 20 games as Liverpool wound up second division champions. A year later in the first division he scored ten in 19 games. At the end of that season he returned to Yorkshire, joining Huddersfield Town for £18,000. Lewis could play on either flank, although he often found himself foraging through the middle and in the end was unlucky to be competing with Ian St John, Ian Callaghan and Peter Thompson for a place up front.

LIDDELL, BILLY. One of the Anfield greats, a name that will forever rank alongside those of Dalglish and Shankly.

Born in Dunfermline, Liddell began his amateur footballing days with Lochgelly Violet, joining Liverpool in
July 1938 when he was still only 16 years old. During the
war he guested with Chelsea and a number of other clubs,
even playing some football in Canada. He mostly, of course,
played with Liverpool where his talents soon became
apparent. Indeed, he was so outstanding that he was chosen
to represent his country in 1942 in a wartime international
against England when he was still only 20. By the end of the
war he had featured in eight wartime internationals. But it
was not until after the war that he made his league debut at
Sheffield United on the last day of August 1946. A week
later he made his Anfield debut, scoring twice as Liverpool
thrashed Chelsea 7–4. From then on his career shot to dizzy
heights. He was capped twice before 1946 was out and went
on to win a total of 28 Scottish caps. By the end of that first
league season Liverpool had clinched the championship.
Sadly it was to be the only honour he would ever win with
Liverpool. He did manage a Cup final outing at Wembley
in 1950 but it was to end in a 2–0 defeat by Arsenal. Despite
the presence of such an outstanding talent Liverpool
struggled through the 1950s, were relegated and found it
hard to win their rightful spot back in division one. And
strangely, it was not until after he had retired that Liverpool
were finally promoted. Liddell's greatest honours came on
the international field where he seemed to be able to
conjure up even greater depths of talent. At a time when
British soccer oozed talented players, Liddell still stood
head and shoulders above most; only Finney and Matthews
were comparable. In 1947 he was chosen to represent Great
Britain in a famous clash against The Rest of Europe at
Hampden Park. Liddell was outstanding, even among such
talent. And in 1955 when the fixture was repeated, this time
in Belfast, Liddell was again chosen. Only he and Matthews
played in both games. Liddell was a rare breed – a two-
footed goalscoring winger who was just as happy to be
lining up at centre-forward as out on one of the wings. It
hardly seemed to matter where he played: he could still

Billy Liddell

antagonise and frustrate defenders. In his first few seasons at Anfield the goals did not come quite so easily but as he moved inside to take over from Albert Stubbins, they began to come more regularly. In the 1949–50 season he managed 20 goals and during Liverpool's first seasons in the second division he caused havoc, hitting 31 goals and 33 the next season. In a career that spanned 537 games he managed an impressive 229 goals, not bad for a player who spent much of his career out on the left-wing. At Liverpool he also established a new club record for appearances (although it has since been broken) and even to this day his tally of 229 goals makes him the fourth highest goalscorer in the club's history. But such statistics alone do not tell the full tale. Liddell was an example to all footballers: professional to the end, always enthusiastic, never complaining. Even when Liverpool were relegated he never thought to ask for a transfer, nor could a lucrative offer from South America tempt him from his beloved Anfield. During the war he served as an RAF navigator and also trained as an accountant. When he retired in 1961 he became a Justice of the Peace and bursar at Liverpool University. Even to this day he is a regular at Liverpool matches. If statues were to be built to footballers, Billy Liddell would be among the first to be so honoured.

LINDSAY, ALEC. Class oozed out of full-back Alec Lindsay. He was rarely ruffled, took everything in his stride and brought a calmness and assuredness to Liverpool's defence throughout the 1970s. Lindsay was a Shankly signing, bought from Bury for £67,000 in March 1969 after having helped his hometown club win promotion to the second division the previous season. Lindsay immediately stepped into the first team at Anfield and went on to make 244 appearances over the next eight seasons. With Chris Lawler at right-back and Lindsay on the left, Liverpool's defence always opted for playing itself out of trouble. There was never any panic, kick out of play or punt upfield to ward off an attack. Lawler and Lindsay always wanted to play football and, like so many Liverpool defenders after them, they would initiate and control many a Liverpool attack. With their authority behind them, the Liverpool midfield could venture forward without too much fear of being caught out by any counter-attack. In September 1975 Lindsay eventually lost his place to a man who played in a similar style, Phil Neal, and moved on to Stoke City. He took with him a league championship medal, a UEFA Cup winners medal and an FA Cup winners' medal. He was also capped four times by England, making his debut in the 2–2 draw with Argentina in 1974. During his Anfield career he netted 18 goals, many of them from the penalty spot.

LITTLEWOODS CUP. See **Football League Cup**.

LIVERMORE, DOUG. Found greater fame as a coach and manager. Born in Liverpool, midfielder Livermore signed for the club in November 1965 but during his five years enjoyed only 13 full league appearances. He left in 1970, joining Norwich for £22,000. He won a second division championship medal there. He later had spells with Bournemouth, Cardiff and Chester before he turned to coaching and has since coached with Cardiff, Norwich, Swansea and Tottenham. Following his appointment as manager Roy Evans invited Livermore to return to Anfield as his assistant. He is now coach to the first team.

LIVERPOOL SENIOR CUP. An annual competition held for many years between the various Merseyside clubs, it was at its height during the 1950s when it was one of the few opportunities for second division Liverpool and first division Everton to face each other. Such rare meetings were contested fiercely with both clubs fielding their first teams. It was often played as a floodlit competition and was won by Liverpool on many occasions.

LIVINGSTONE, GEORGE. Inside-right signed from Celtic in May 1902. Livingstone had just one season at

Anfield, making 31 league appearances and scoring just four goals. He moved to Manchester City in May 1903 where, playing alongside Billy Meredith, he won an FA Cup winners' medal. He later played with Glasgow Rangers and Manchester United and went on to coach at Ibrox. He was capped twice by Scotland though never while with Liverpool.

LLOYD, CLIFF. Cliff Lloyd had only a relatively short spell at Anfield, joining the club as a full-back in 1936, but failing to make any appearances. The war interrupted his career although he did guest for Wrexham, Fulham and Brentford. After the war he continued playing for Fulham and later coached in Norway. He finally moved to Bristol Rovers for a season during the early 1950s. He was to become better known as the secretary of the Professional Footballers' Association, the players' union. He became secretary in 1953 and retired in 1982.

LLOYD, LARRY. During the late 1960s and the 1970s it was unusual for a player leaving Liverpool to go on to greater glory. But Larry Lloyd was the exception to the rule. Born in Bristol, his early footballing was with Bristol Rovers before Liverpool stepped in with a £50,000 offer in April 1969 that tempted him north. Lloyd was an immediate hit, the perfect replacement for Kop favourite Ron Yeats. He was not unlike Yeats either – massive, powerful and inspiring calm in those around him. He did well at Anfield, winning a first division championship medal in 1973 and a UEFA Cup winners' medal the same year. Then as Bob Paisley took over as manager Lloyd was surprisingly sold for £225,000 to Coventry City. He had played 217 games for Liverpool. Two years later and with his career appearing to be on the slide, he was transferred to Nottingham Forest for the knockdown price of £60,000. Coventry must have been kicking themselves as Brian Clough resurrected the young man's career. Within a season Forest were champions and Lloyd went on to claim two European Cup medals and two Football League Cup medals with his new club. He left Forest in March 1981 to become player-manager at Wigan Athletic. He was later manager at Notts County. While he was at Liverpool Lloyd was capped just three times by England, making his debut in the goalless draw against Wales in 1971. Nine years later, when he was at Forest, he was recalled for a fourth cap. But it ended in disaster with Lloyd booked, injured and substituted as well as scoring what looked like an own goal. England lost 4–1; it was his last international honour.

LOCK, FRANK. Full-back with 41 league appearances during the early 1950s. Lock came from Charlton Athletic in December 1953 along with his Charlton colleague John Evans in a desperate attempt to help stave off relegation. It was unsuccessful and Lock saw the remainder of his Anfield days in the second division. He joined Watford in June 1955.

LONGEST GAME. Liverpool have been involved in two extraordinarily long cup-ties, both semi-finals and both occasions on which Liverpool eventually lost. The first in 1899 was against Sheffield United. The first match was drawn 2–2 and the second 4 – 4. The third game, played at Fallowfield in Manchester, was abandoned with Liverpool winning 1–0 when fans kept spilling on to the pitch. United won the fourth game 1–0. Receipts for the four matches were £3,156, a world record at the time. In 1980 Liverpool had another four-match semi-final, this time against Arsenal. The first game was drawn 0–0, while the second and third matches ended one goal apiece. Arsenal then won the fourth contest 1–0. It had taken 420 minutes to settle the tie.

LONGWORTH, EPHRAIM. Regarded by many as one of the finest full-backs of the inter-war years, Longworth came to Anfield from Leyton, then playing in the Southern League, in 1910 and played the remainder of his career with

Liverpool. He could play either on the right or left of defence with equal fluency and was automatic choice to captain the side. He was also the first Liverpool player to captain England and went on to win five caps. He made his debut for England in 1920 when they beat Scotland in one of the most memorable internationals of all time as England fought back from being 4–2 behind to win by the odd goal in nine. Already 32 years old then, he made his final appearance for England at the age of 35, also against Scotland. Captain of Liverpool's two championship-winning sides of the early 1920s, he had earlier played in the 1914 FA Cup final when Liverpool lost 1–0 to Burnley. Born in Bolton, Longworth began his footballing days with Bolton Wanderers in 1907. When he retired from playing in 1928 he took up a coaching position at Anfield and continued to serve the club for many years. By then he had played a total of 370 games for Liverpool but failed to ever score a goal for the club.

LOW, NORMAN. Although centre-half Norman Low played just 13 league games for Liverpool, he will be best remembered at the club as their chief scout, a position he held between 1965 and 1967. Born in 1914, Low came from a distinguished footballing family. He began his own career as an amateur with Newcastle United, joining Liverpool in October 1933. He stayed for just three years before moving on to Newport County. He guested with both Everton and Liverpool during the war and then enjoyed spells as manager at Norwich City, Workington and Port Vale before taking up his scouting post at Anfield.

LOWE, HENRY. Known to the fans as Harry Lowe, he joined Liverpool after playing against them with Gainsbor-ough Trinity in the 1911 FA Cup. He moved straight into the side as a half-back and over the next five seasons played 135 games. He ought to have captained the side in the 1914 FA Cup final but injury robbed him of his place and Liverpool of his steadying influence. The outbreak of the

First World War further robbed him of appearances and after the war he managed just five more games before moving on to Nottingham Forest in 1920.

LUCAS, TOM. Another Liverpool player who was to wind up as captain of England, Lucas was a popular full-back from St Helens who was on Manchester United's books when Liverpool snapped him up in 1916. He was to prove a fine signing, playing 366 times for the club between 1919 and 1932. He was a regular member of the side that clinched the league championship in 1922 but was unfortunately kept out of the championship side of the following season by Ephraim Longworth. After that he won his place back as the team was reshuffled to accommodate McKinlay, Longworth and Lucas. He missed few games in the seasons that followed until he moved on to Clapton Orient in 1933. He won his first England cap in October 1921 and then his third and final cap when he captained his country as England beat Belgium 5–3 in May 1926.

M

MACs, TEAM OF THE ALL. Liverpool's first ever team was known as the 'Team of the all Macs' because there were no fewer than nine players on the club's books during their first season with surnames which began with Mac. And all but one of the team that turned out for Liverpool against Rotherham had been born in Scotland.

McBAIN, NEIL. Scottish full-back Neil McBain may have made only a few appearances for Liverpool during the late 1920s but his principal claim to fame is as the oldest player to turn out for a league club. That was in March 1947 when, at the age of 52, he appeared in goal for New Brighton in a third division north match. He was manager of New Brighton at the time; they lost 3–0. During his long career McBain also played for Everton, Manchester United and Ayr. He was also a well-travelled manager with stints at Luton, Ayr, Watford, Leyton Orient, New Brighton and Estudiantes de la Plata of Argentina.

McDERMOTT, TERRY. Kirkby-born McDermott some-how escaped the Merseyside net and instead joined Bury as an apprentice, making 83 appearances for the Shakers

Terry McDermott

before joining Newcastle United. He appeared for New-castle in the 1974 Cup final when they were beaten by Liverpool but clearly impressed enough for Liverpool to sign him six months later. At Anfield all his enthusiasm finally came to maturity as he went on to make 310 appearances and win a crop of honours. He was an aggressive, hard-running midfielder who contributed 75 goals, eagerly snatching up loose opportunities. He also had a spectacular ability to volley the ball which resulted in some memorable goals and his final goal against Spurs in the 7–0 thrashing of the London side in September 1978 is remembered as perhaps the finest Anfield has ever seen – though more for the slick build-up than the clinical finish. McDermott won three European Cup medals with Liver-pool as well as four league titles. In 1980 he became the first player to ever win the PFA and the Football Writers' awards for Player of the Year. Capped 25 times by England, he finally left Liverpool in September 1983, returning to Newcastle in a £100,000 deal. He later played for Cork and Apoel of Cyprus but went back to Newcastle as assistant manager to Kevin Keegan in 1992.

McDONALD, KEVIN. Bought from Leicester in Novem-ber 1984 for £400,000, McDonald never quite made the grade at Anfield. He had been bought as a potential replacement for Graeme Souness and might have gone on to become a permanent fixture but a broken leg brought his Liverpool career to a sad end. He was a tall, gangly player in the mould of a Phil Thompson but lacking the former Liverpool captain's durability. He eventually returned to Leicester City.

McDOUGALL, JIMMY. Outstanding half-back who cap-tained both Liverpool and Scotland during the 1930s. McDougall was signed from Partick Thistle in 1928 and went on to play 357 games for the Reds. He began his Anfield career as an inside-forward but in a move owing more to necessity than inspiration, he was converted into a half-back. Alongside fellow Scots Matt Busby and Tiny Bradshaw he went on to play as a left-half over the next ten years in what was to become one of the finest half-back lines Liverpool have ever boasted. He was capped twice by Scotland, captaining the side on both occasions. Unfortunately they lost both games, the first 5–0 against the outstanding Austrians and the second 3–0 against the Italians in a game watched by Mussolini. Before the start of that game the Italian dictator had handed a bouquet of flowers to the somewhat astonished Scottish captain, McDougall.

McGARVEY, FRANK. The striker who never made it. Signed from St Mirren in 1979 for a huge fee of £250,000, McGarvey was a proven marksman when he arrived at Anfield, having scored 80 goals in something like 180 games for St Mirren. Much was expected of him. He was a hot property, with Arsenal, Aston Villa and even Ajax all chasing the young man. He won two Scottish caps while at Anfield, adding to the glut of Under-21 honours he had already won. But success at an international level meant little to Liverpool and with Dalglish, Johnson, McDermott and Case around, McGarvey never even managed a first team outing. Eventually he returned to Scotland, joining Glasgow Celtic for £250,000. He was to enjoy more success there.

McGUIGAN, ANDY. Although Andy McGuigan played only two seasons for Liverpool he can lay claim to fame on two counts. He was the first ever Liverpool player to hit five goals in a league match. And second, he was a member of Liverpool's first championship side. Born in Newton Stewart in 1878, he signed for Liverpool from Hibernian in 1900. He made 14 appearances in the title-winning side of 1900–01, scoring 14 goals, and then made 21 appearances the following season. His five goals in a match came in January 1902 at Anfield when Stoke City, suffering from food poisoning, were at one stage reduced to seven men, as players regularly left the field to make a call. Liverpool ran amok, hitting seven goals. At the end of that season McGuigan joined Middlesbrough and later played with Accrington Stanley and Exeter. He returned to Liverpool as a trainer and was associated with the side that won two championships in the early 1920s.

McINNES, JIMMY. Former player who became secretary of the club. McInnes joined Liverpool from Third Lanark in 1938 but only played for one season before war was declared and the Football League put into mothballs. During the war, however, he guested with Brighton, Newcastle, York, Leeds, Manchester United, QPR and Fulham. After the war he retired and joined the club's administrative staff, initially becoming assistant secretary and then secretary in 1955, a post he held until his death in 1965 when he committed suicide. He was a graduate of Edinburgh University with a BSc degree.

McKENNA, JOHN. One of the most distinguished names in football administration and the first ever Liverpool manager, though he combined this with the job of club secretary. McKenna was a close colleague of John Houlding and after the split with Everton Houlding asked McKenna to take over the day-to-day running of the club and to find him a new team. McKenna duly obliged and began his recruitment drive north of the border, signing up almost an entire team of Scots. McKenna was a self-made Irishman, born in Ulster in May 1854, who came to Liverpool as a nine-year-old. He began his working life running errands for a grocer's shop but soon rose to become a prominent businessman. In 1896 he signed up Tom Watson, the highly successful manager of league champions Sunderland, to take over as manager at Anfield. McKenna then concentrated on an administrative career in football. He was not only a director of Liverpool until 1922 but from 1910 until his death in March 1936 was President of the Football League, the longest ever serving president.

McKINLAY, DON. Scottish international who captained Liverpool to two consecutive championships. Born near Glasgow, McKinlay was snapped up by Liverpool before any Football League or Scottish League club had realised his outstanding talent. McKinlay was to repay Liverpool their faith and investment with 433 appearances over almost 20 seasons. He made his league debut towards the end of the 1909–10 campaign and pulled on a red shirt for the final time at the beginning of the 1928 season. Although McKinlay was essentially a defender he enjoyed nothing more than the occasional burst into the opposition area; it was a tactic that paid off with 34 goals and a great many more assists. He was almost a play-anywhere player, equally at home as a half-back or inside-forward. McKinlay *was* Liverpool and their two league triumphs of the early 1920s were due to his inspiring leadership as much as anything. McKinlay was capped twice by Scotland, both caps coming in 1912, but after the war, when he was probably at his most effective, he was surprisingly ignored by the Scottish selectors. McKinlay would have made many more appearances for Liverpool had the First World War not intervened and had his career not been cut short by injury. But on any scale his 400-odd appearances place him among the club's finest ever servants.

McMAHON, STEVE. The one-time Everton regular initially turned down a move to Liverpool, preferring instead to join Aston Villa. However, his career in the Midlands lasted only 18 months and he returned to Merseyside in September 1985, this time settling for Liverpool in a £350,000 deal. McMahon was Kenny Dalglish's first signing and he proved to be one of his most astute. McMahon brought a presence and aggression to Liverpool's midfield that had been sorely lacking since the departure of Graeme Souness. Strong, hard-tackling and a fine distributor of the ball, McMahon soon became the engine around which the Liverpool midfield fired. His success at Liverpool also brought him England honours

Steve McMahon

Steve McManaman

with 17 caps, including a trip to Italia '90. McMahon also picked up league championship and FA Cup honours at Anfield. The resignation of Kenny Dalglish as Liverpool manager and the subsequent arrival of Graeme Souness brought his Anfield career to a premature end and in 1991 he was transferred to Manchester City for £900,000. There he joined his former Everton colleague and City manager Peter Reid.

McMANAMAN, STEVE. Local-born winger who made the breakthrough into first team football at the beginning of 1991–92 season. Tall, lanky and fast, McManaman was an instant hit, taking over from the injured John Barnes. He had already been capped by the England Under-21 side even before he had made his league debut. During the 1992 Cup final against Sunderland McManaman switched wings at half-time and had a dramatic effect on the game, turning the Sunderland defence inside out and contributing significantly to Liverpool's victory. The following season McManaman's game went into decline but during the 1994–95 season his old skills and ability returned. Returning to Wembley for the Coca-Cola Cup final he swung the game in Liverpool's favour with two astonishing individual goals as he turned the Bolton defence inside out. He was also capped by England and by the end of the season was one of the most talked about players in the Premiership.

McMULLAN, DAVID. Over the years Liverpool have boasted surprisingly few Northern Ireland internationals but one who did make the grade was David McMullan. Born in Belfast, he signed for Liverpool in 1925 and remained with them for three years, making 21 league appearances as a half-back. In July 1928 he joined the New York Giants but within a year was back playing for Belfast Celtic. He was capped three times for Northern Ireland while at Anfield.

McNAB, JOCK. Tall, willowy half-back who made 200

league appearances for Liverpool during the 1920s. He was a member of the side that won two championships. Born in Scotland, he joined Liverpool from Bellshill Athletic in November 1919 but had to wait a couple of years before he secured his spot in the team. Capped by Scotland just once, against Wales in 1923, he was transferred to Queen's Park Rangers in June 1928.

McOWEN, BILL. Goalkeeper who conceded just 16 goals as Liverpool won the second division title in 1894, their first season in league football. Signed from Blackburn Rovers, he left Liverpool after one season to continue his career as a dentist but had a later spell with Blackpool as an amateur. He made just 23 league appearances for Liverpool and was the only Englishman among so many 'Macs'.

McPHERSON, ARCHIE. Inside-forward who found greater fame away from Anfield. He came to Liverpool from Glasgow Rangers in November 1929 and went on to make 130 league appearances, scoring 18 goals. In December 1934 he joined Sheffield United and appeared in the 1936 Cup final. After the war he managed Alloa Athletic.

McQUE, JOE. Joe McQue was one of the original 'team of the all Macs'. A tall, distinguished centre-half, he joined Liverpool from Glasgow Celtic in 1892 and went on to make 122 appearances, helping Liverpool to two second division championships. He played in Liverpool's first ever match and also in their first Football League fixture.

McQUEEN, MATT. Former player and manager and one of the outstanding names of Liverpool's early history. He was recruited in 1892, played in all Liverpool's early fixtures and was a member of the side that won two second division titles. He appeared in at least half a dozen positions for Liverpool, including goal where he made more than a dozen appearances. Yet he was equally adept as a winger, inside-forward and a half-back and could play on either flank. Over six seasons he made 87 appearances but scored just one goal. He was capped twice by Scotland while he was playing with Leith Athletic. He retired in 1899 to take up even more footballing appointments, first as a league referee. In 1918 he was appointed a director of Liverpool and then in 1923 when David Ashworth sensationally quit, McQueen took over as manager. He was fortunate in that Ashworth's team was well on its way to a second successive championship. Times became slightly more difficult after that but McQueen showed considerable talent in the transfer market with some fine signings including Gordon Hodgson, Arthur Riley and Jimmy Jackson. However, McQueen's reign as manager was prematurely ended when he lost a leg in a car accident while returning from a scouting mission to Sheffield. He persevered for a while but in February 1928 he was eventually forced to retire. For many years he lived in the Kemlyn Road, next door to Anfield.

McVEAN, MALCOLM. The scorer of Liverpool's first ever league goal and another famous member of the 'team of the all Macs'. Signed from Third Lanark, he played 94 league games, scoring 24 goals before his transfer to Burnley.

MAIN STAND. Built in 1973 to replace the old timber stand with the red and white gable that had been constructed in 1895. It was officially opened by HRH the Duke of Kent and has a capacity of 8,771.

MANAGER OF THE YEAR. Over the past 25 years Liverpool managers have been remarkably successful in carrying off the Manager of the Year awards. Bill Shankly was the first recipient when he was named Manager of the Year in 1973 and was named Manager of the Month on seven occasions. Bob Paisley collected 22 monthly awards and was Manager of the Year no fewer than a record six times (1976, 1977, 1979, 1980, 1982 and 1983). Joe Fagan picked up three monthly awards and the Manager of the

Year award for 1984. Kenny Dalglish won the trophy in 1986, 1988 and 1990.

MANAGERS. In a 100-year history Liverpool Football Club have had only 14 managers. And in the past 50 years they have had only nine, one of the lowest numbers in the Football League. They have been as follows:
1892–96 John McKenna and W. E. Barclay
1896–1915 Tom Watson
1920–23 David Ashworth
1923–28 Matt McQueen
1928–36 George Patterson
1936–51 George Kay
1951–56 Don Welsh
1956–59 Phil Taylor
1959–74 Bill Shankly
1974–83 Bob Paisley
1983–85 Joe Fagan
1985–91 Kenny Dalglish
1991–94 Graeme Souness
1994–   Roy Evans

MARATHON. For many years prior to the Second World War and even for a few years after the war had ended, Anfield was the finishing point of the Liverpool marathon. After a race around the city the runners traditionally finished their 26 miles with a lap of the Anfield pitch.

MARATHON MATCHES. Liverpool have been involved in a number of Cup games that have gone to three matches but only two which have ever gone to four meetings. That was in 1899 when Liverpool faced Sheffield United in the FA Cup semi-final. The first game was played at Nottingham where the two teams shared four goals. A few days later they met at Bolton and drew 4–4. The third game was played at Fallowfield in Manchester. A crowd of 30,000 turned up, far too many for the ground, and at half-time, with Sheffield leading 1–0 and the crowd spilling on to the pitch, the referee wisely decided to abandon proceedings for fear of safety. The fourth game was played at Derby a few days later with Sheffield United eventually winning 1–0. In 1980 Liverpool played four games against Arsenal in the semi-final of the FA Cup. The first game ended in a goalless draw at Hillsborough. In the second game at Villa Park the two teams drew 1–1. There was an identical scoreline in the third game, also at Villa Park. In the fourth game Arsenal eventually won 1–0 at Highfield Road. Just under 170,000 had watched the four games which had lasted 420 minutes. Another interesting marathon came during the 1983–84 season when it took Liverpool 13 matches to win the Milk Cup. Although some of the games were played on a two-legged basis, Liverpool managed to draw all their other games, including the final against Everton before they eventually lifted the trophy.

MARKSMEN, LEAGUE. Liverpool's top league goalscorer is Roger Hunt who struck 245 league goals during his 11 years at Anfield. Only nine players have hit more than 100 league goals for the club.
1. Roger Hunt 245
2. Gordon Hodgson 232
3. Ian Rush 224
4. Billy Liddell 216
5. Harry Chambers 135
6. Jack Parkinson 123
7. Sam Raybould 119
8. Kenny Dalglish 118
9. Dick Forshaw 117
10. Jack Balmer 99

MARKSMEN, OVERALL. A dozen players have hit a century of goals for Liverpool. The club's top marksman is now Ian Rush who recently overhauled Roger Hunt's long standing record.
The Century Club
1. Ian Rush 339

MARSH, MIKE. Kirkby youngster who made the break-through into Liverpool's first team during the 1991–92 season. He made his first league appearance as a substitute in March 1989 but with so many talented players around Anfield he was forced to wait until injury to first-teamers gave him his opportunity. A neat midfielder with plenty of running who likes to go forward, Marsh has also had spells in the Liverpool defence. In September 1993 Graeme Souness sold him to West Ham United along with David Burrows in a deal that brought Julian Dicks to Anfield.

MATTEO, DOMINIC. Dumfries-born midfielder who has made only a few appearances for the club. Matteo was spotted by manager Kenny Dalglish when he went to see his own son playing one afternoon. Dalglish was so impressed by Matteo that he offered him a chance at Anfield. He made his debut against Manchester City in October 1993 and although he has yet to win a regular place he is still young and regarded as one for the future.

MATTHEWS, ROBERT. Welsh international centre-forward with just nine league appearances for Liverpool even though he scored four goals. He joined Liverpool from Welsh junior football just after the end of the First World War but failed to hold his place in the first team and was eventually transferred to Bristol City. While at Liverpool he won his first Welsh cap and later added two more caps to his name.

MELIA, JIMMY. Ever popular inside-left of the 1950s. Born in Liverpool, Melia joined the Anfield staff in 1953 and made his league debut two years later. Capped at schoolboy and youth level, he eventually won a full England cap in 1963 and gained a second cap later that year as England beat Switzerland 8–1 in Basle with Melia scoring. It was to be his final cap. Melia was a useful inside-forward, always prepared to try and carry the ball into the area. Unfortunately most of his football was played in the lower leagues with his best season in 1961–62 as Liverpool took the second division title. Life in the first division was harder and after a couple of seasons he lost his place and was transferred to Wolves for £55,000. His career then took him in numerous directions, playing with Wolves, Southampton and Aldershot before trying his hand at management with Crewe and Southport as well as in the Middle East and in the United States. He returned to England and in a brief spell as manager of Brighton took them to a Wembley Cup final. He later worked in Portugal. He played 287 games for Liverpool, scoring 78 goals.

MELWOOD. Liverpool's training ground in West Derby, Liverpool.

MILK CUP. See **FOOTBALL LEAGUE CUP.**

MILLER, TOM. Centre-forward of the Edwardian era who came from a large footballing family. His brother John also played for Liverpool, while four of his cousins appeared for Hamilton Academicals. Tom himself had played for the Accies before joining Liverpool in February 1912. Over the next eight years he made 146 appearances, scoring 58 goals, although his career was badly interrupted by the First World War. He appeared in the 1914 Cup final for Liverpool and was one of a number of players suspended by the FA after being involved in the rigging of a game against Manchester United on Good Friday 1915. Ironically Miller left Liverpool in 1920 to join, of all clubs, Manchester United. Miller's best season came in 1913–14 when he struck 16 league goals, yet for a centre-forward his goalscoring record was hardly impressive. He was capped once for Scotland while at Anfield and won a couple more honours while at United.

MILNE, GORDON. Bill Shankly had known Gordon Milne since he was a toddler, having played with his father Jimmy during his days at Preston. It was hardly surprising then that Shankly knew what he was buying when he paid Preston £16,000 for the services of young Gordon in August 1960. Milne soon became a permanent fixture in the Liverpool midfield and was a key member of the second division winning side. In seven seasons at Anfield he made 277 appearances, scoring 19 goals, and was as popular a player as any. He picked up a championship medal in 1964 but unfortunately missed the FA Cup final the following year through injury. He was capped 14 times by England but did not feature in Alf Ramsey's World Cup team. Quiet but effective, he left Liverpool in May 1967, joining Blackpool for £30,000. In 1970 he became player-manager of Wigan and then had successful spells as manager of Coventry and Leicester as well as running the England youth team. In 1986 he moved to Turkey as manager of Besiktas.

MOLBY, JAN. The Great Dane Jan Molby joined Liverpool from the famous Dutch club Ajax in August 1984 for just £200,000. Since then he has gone on to make more than 230 appearances with 50 goals to his credit. On a number of occasions it seemed his Anfield career was at an end but various transfer deals fell through and Molby remained, usually to regain his place. At one point it seemed he was destined for Barcelona but the deal collapsed when Molby could not agree terms. A superb passer of the ball who on his day was as good as anyone in Europe, he also possessed

Jan Molby

a fierce free kick which brought Liverpool numerous goals. Dalglish occasionally used him as a sweeper, a tactic that had mixed results, as Molby was not always the surest of tacklers. He made his debut for Liverpool in August 1984 against Norwich. Born in Kolding in Denmark, Molby has played on a number of occasions for his country. During his Anfield career Molby picked up two league championship medals and two FA Cup winners' medals.

MOLYNEUX, JOHN. Right full-back during Liverpool's

dismal second division days of the 1950s. Although he was always popular, Molyneux was hardly an outstanding defender and it was not surprising that Shankly should discard his services in favour of Gerry Byrne. He made only three appearances during the 1961–62 season and at the end of that season rejoined Chester. In all he played 249 games for the Reds.

MORAN, RONNIE. One of the finest servants Liverpool Football Club has ever known, he has been associated with the club in almost every capacity. Liverpool-born, he came to Anfield in 1951 as a 17-year-old, making his league debut in November 1952. He went on to make 379 appearances, scoring 16 goals in a league career that spanned 13 seasons. The vast majority of his football was played in the second division but he was a regular member of the side that won promotion in 1962. He played just a couple of seasons in the first division before finally giving way to younger talents. A strong, sturdy defender, Moran's experience was vital during Liverpool's early years back in the first division. He then retired to the Liverpool bootroom, becoming reserve team trainer in 1972 and later first team coach. As Joe Fagan's number two many expected him to take over when Fagan retired but instead he was overlooked in favour of Kenny Dalglish. When Dalglish resigned as manager in February 1991 Moran temporarily took control but a poor run of results not only cost Liverpool the title but almost certainly cost Moran the chance of becoming manager.

MORGAN, HUGH. Scottish international who joined Liverpool in 1898 from St Mirren. An inside-left, he netted 15 goals in 59 league appearances. He won a second and final Scottish cap while on Liverpool's books and was transferred to Blackburn Rovers in June 1900.

MORRIS, RICHARD. Welsh international who played with Liverpool during the early years of this century. He left the club in 1902 after 38 league appearances to join Leeds City, and later played with Plymouth and Huddersfield.

MORRISON, TOM. Pre-war Scottish international. Morrison was transferred to Liverpool for £4,000 in November 1927 from St Mirren and remained at Anfield for eight years before joining Sunderland. The following season he won a league championship medal with the Roker Park club. Most of his Anfield football was played as a half-back although at Sunderland he was converted into a full-back. Morrison notched up 254 appearances for Liverpool and played for Scotland against England in 1927 when he was still with St Mirren. He also won a Scottish Cup winners' medal with St Mirren.

N

NEAL, PHIL. Phil Neal was Bob Paisley's first signing, joining Liverpool in October 1974 from fourth division Northampton Town for £60,000. He was to prove a bargain and went on to play more than 600 games for the club, scoring 60 goals, many of them from the penalty spot. Neal was in the typical mould of a modern Liverpool full-back – willowy, fast and boasting a well-timed tackle. Few defenders ever got the better of him though he has probably never been given the full credit for his part in the outstanding achievements of the late 1970s and 1980s. Neal was the fulcrum of the team, with so many moves upfield beginning with him and involving him as the ball was steadily carried forward. Even then he would be chasing down the flanks looking to get inside the penalty area himself to try his luck at goal. He made his first appearance in November 1974 and soon began to settle into the side. Over the next ten seasons he missed just one league game until the appointment of Dalglish as player-manager. Dalglish's appointment spelled the end of Neal's days. He had half-expected the job himself and when Dalglish stripped him of the captaincy he knew his days were numbered. There was some bitterness when he left but it would be wrong to allow

Phil Neal

that to interfere with any assessment of Neal as player and captain. During his spell at Anfield he became one of the most honoured players in European football, the winner of four European Cup medals, one UEFA Cup medal, seven league titles, and four Football League Cup winners' medals. The only medal to elude him was an FA Cup winners'. On top of that he was capped 50 times by

England. He joined Bolton Wanderers as player-manager in December 1985 but was unlucky to miss out on promotion a number of times and in the summer of 1992 he was sacked. He soon found employment elsewhere and was also appointed as an assistant to the England team manager Graham Taylor.

NEIL, ROBERT. Scottish centre-half who had just one season with Liverpool. His early career was with Hibernian but he joined Liverpool in May 1896 and featured in 23 games the following season, scoring two goals. He was already a Scottish international when he arrived at Anfield but failed to add to his honours. He left Liverpool at the end of his first and only season, returning to Scotland to join Glasgow Rangers. He won two further Scottish caps during his seven years at Ibrox and four Scottish league championships as well as the Scottish Cup.

NICHOLL, JAMES. Jimmy Nicholl played in Liverpool's FA Cup final side of 1914, having been with the club just a few months. A left-footed player, he preferred to play on the wing or at inside-forward. He joined Liverpool from Middlesbrough but the outbreak of war brought his career to a halt.

NICKNAME. Liverpool's nickname is usually 'the Reds' or 'the Pool'.

NICOL, STEVE. If you had to name an all-time Liverpool team, you can be sure that the name of Steve Nicol would feature somewhere in the discussions. Indeed, the *Rothmans Football Year Book* of 1989 named him as a substitute for their team of best British internationals of the previous 20 years. A tough, resilient right-back, Nicol joined Liverpool from Ayr United in October 1981. He cost £300,000 but nobody had any doubts that he would be worth every penny. And so it proved. He had a long apprenticeship in the Central League and although he made his first team debut in August 1982 he did not become a regular until the following season. Since then he has played over 300 league games for the club. During the 1990–91 season he played in almost every position as injuries caused havoc with team selection. Always reliable, Nicol won a then record 14 Scottish caps at Under-21 level. He won his first full cap against Yugoslavia in 1985 and has gone on to collect 27 caps. In 1989 he was named Footballer of the Year. He was a substitute in the 1984 European Cup final and has won a glut of domestic honours including championship and FA Cup final medals. In 1994 Nicol joined Notts County.

Steve Nicol

Berry Nieuwenhuys

NIEUWENHUYS, BERRY. The South African winger was always better known as 'Nivvy' as nobody could pronounce his name. He was one of many South Africans who came to play for the club during the 1930s, most of them recruited after the South African touring team had made one of their regular trips to Great Britain. Nivvy was to become one of the most prominent of all the recruits, turning out on more than 250 occasions in a red shirt. He also scored 79 goals in an Anfield career that lasted until 1947. But like so many players of the period he would no doubt have proven an even more valuable player had war not intervened to rob him of his most productive years. During his final season he made 15 appearances as Liverpool clinched the first division title; he even managed five goals. But it was to be his only honour at Anfield and after that he retired and returned home to South Africa. He could play equally effectively on either wing and was renowned for his powerful shot.

O

OGRIZOVIC, STEVE. Liverpool's reserve goalkeeper over a period of five years. At 6ft 5in Ogrizovic was one of the tallest 'keepers in the Football League but with Ray Clemence the number one choice Ogrizovic's chances were restricted to just four league appearances. Known to the fans as 'Oggie', he followed in the footpath of another famous Anfield goalkeeper, Sam Hardy, who had also come to Liverpool from Chesterfield. Eventually he decided to try his luck elsewhere and was exchanged for the Shrewsbury Town goalkeeper, Bob Wardle, who unfortunately had to retire within the year. Shrewsbury clearly got the better of the deal with Ogrizovic quickly becoming a regular in their side before he was sold to Coventry for £72,500. At Coventry he has enjoyed deserved success, winning an FA Cup winners' medal with them in 1987.

OLYMPICS. During the Edwardian era Liverpool boasted a player with two Olympic gold medals. He was Arthur Berry who won both his medals with the Great Britain soccer side in the 1908 and 1912 games. Berry had a couple of spells with Liverpool before the First World War but made only four league appearances. Joe Dines was another Liverpool player who also the holder of an Olympic gold medal, having represented Great Britain at soccer in the 1912 Olympics. Dines made just one appearance for Liverpool in 1912 and was killed in action during the First World War on the Western Front.

ORR, ROBERT. Came to Liverpool in April 1908 with a massive reputation. Already a Scottish international, he had helped Newcastle United to two league championships and an FA Cup final appearance. Yet despite his reputation and unquestionable talents Orr never got on very well with the Tyneside fans and Newcastle sold him while there was still plenty of life in him. He subsequently enjoyed four good seasons at Anfield, making 108 appearances and scoring 35 goals. He was Liverpool's top scorer in 1908–09 with 20 goals out of a team total of 57 goals. He left in January 1912, returning north to join Raith Rovers. An inside-forward or winger who usually operated on the left, Orr stood only 5ft 5in but weighed in at eleven and a half stones. He was capped twice by Scotland while at Newcastle.

ORRELL, JOHN. Liverpool brewer, of Orrell's Brewery, who originally owned the Anfield ground. It was Orrell's demands for alterations to the ground and then his decision to increase the rent that led to most of the members of Everton Football Club leaving Anfield, which in turn led to the eventual formation of Liverpool Football Club.

OVERSEAS PLAYERS. Prior to the 1980s Liverpool's overseas players were all South Africans but in 1979 they added a new dimension to their collection with the signing of Israeli Avi Cohen. Since then the club has boasted a number of continental players. The first of these was Jan Molby, the Danish international who came to Anfield in 1984. He was to be joined in 1992 by another Dane, Torben Piechnik. That same year the Norwegian Stig Bjornebye was signed. Ronnie Rosenthal, another Israeli international, joined the club in 1990.

P

PAGNAM, FRED. Liverpool forward of the Edwardian era. Pagnam was something of a well-travelled player. He began his football with his local club, Blackpool, and then progressed to The Wednesday, Huddersfield Town, Southport Central, Blackpool again, Liverpool, Arsenal and Cardiff before ending his days with Watford. He joined Liverpool just as the First World War broke out and would without question have made many more league appearances for the club than his meagre 37 had war not interrupted his playing days. He was a brave little striker who netted 28 goals in his 37 games. During the war years he even managed 42 goals in 48 games. In 1919 Liverpool sold him to Arsenal where he continued to hit the back of the net at the rate of a goal every other game. He eventually became manager of Watford and saw his footballing years out as manager of the Turkish national side and then as a coach in Holland.

PAISLEY, BOB. Liverpool manager and player. Bob Paisley had a solid career as a player with Liverpool rather than a spectacular one. The glitter and the rave notices were to come later when he became manager. He joined the club in

Bob Paisley

1939 from Bishop Auckland after he had helped them win the FA Amateur Cup but he did not make his league debut until after the war. During the intervening years he served in the army and played some wartime games for Liverpool but, like so many players, his best years had probably gone by the time peace returned. He did, however, make 33 league appearances for the Reds as they stormed to the league championship in the first season after the war. He was a tough, little left-half, always full of running, with a never-say-die attitude and a crisp tackle. In 1950 it was Paisley who scored the all-important first goal against Everton in the FA Cup semi-final at Maine Road that set Liverpool on the road to Wembley. Unfortunately when Wembley came around there was no place for Paisley, who had been deputising for the injured Laurie Hughes. It was a lesson he would heed.

After 278 games Paisley retired in 1954 and took a job on the Liverpool training staff assisting manager Phil Taylor. He became a qualified physiotherapist and when Bill Shankly arrived in 1959 Paisley became his number two. The rest is history. Paisley took over from Shankly in 1974, telling his players at their first get-together that he never really wanted the job. But that was no doubt just a touch of the famed Paisley canniness. If he didn't want the job he certainly did not show it when it came to winning. His record as a manager was second to none: in a nine-year spell as boss of Anfield he won three European Cups, six league championships, three League Cups in succession and the UEFA Cup. The only trophy to elude him was the FA Cup. He was also voted Manager of the Year on six occasions and was awarded the OBE. In short, Bob Paisley is undoubtedly the most successful manager in the history of the Football League and probably the most successful in the history of British soccer. When he retired in 1983 with yet another trophy, he was appointed a director of the club. It is impossible to fathom the secret of Paisley's success, but judging by the number of outstanding players who passed through Anfield during his time, it has to be argued that he had more than a good eye for a player. Perhaps therein lies the secret. He retired as a club director in January 1992 due to ill health.

PARKINSON, JACK. Jack Parkinson's early Anfield career was thwarted by the presence of Sam Raybould, one of the most prolific goalscorers of the era. And it was not until Parkinson was played alongside Raybould, rather than as his replacement, that his career really began to take off. He was a regular member of the 1905 side that clinched the second division championship but played only a handful of games the following season due to injury as Liverpool lifted the first division title. He had joined Liverpool at the turn of the century and remained with them until the outbreak of the First World War, playing 222 games and scoring a remarkable 128 goals. Raybould was also scoring at a similar rate which must have made the Liverpool pair the most feared striking partnership of the period.

PARRY, EDWARD. Welsh international defender who had five years with Liverpool during the early 1920s. Although they were highly successful seasons for the club, Parry never enjoyed much of that success, making only a dozen or so appearances. But if his talents generally went unrewarded at Anfield, they were at least recognised by his country, who capped him five times during his Anfield career.

PARRY, MAURICE. Welsh international half-back who went on to coach some of the greatest clubs in football. Parry came to Anfield in March 1900 and remained for nine years before joining Partick Thistle. In that time he made 221 appearances, picking up second division and league championship medals. He was capped 16 times by Wales while he was with Liverpool. After Partick Thistle he became manager of Rotherham County and then in 1921 he joined Barcelona as coach. He later coached with Frankfurt and Cologne before returning to Anfield as a coach. His son, Frank Parry, played for Everton during the early 1930s.

PATTERSON, GEORGE. Liverpool manager during the inter-war years. Although Patterson did not boast much of a playing career, he eventually rose to become a highly respected manager. He came to the club in 1908 as an assistant to the great Tom Watson. When Watson died in 1915 Patterson was immediately promoted to club secretary and during the war he handled most of the club's affairs. After the war, however, the club decided to split the job of secretary and manager, appointing David Ashworth as the new team manager. Then in 1928 the club reversed its policy and Patterson was formally appointed as secretary-manager. His managerial career began well with high positions during his first few seasons and a team that boasted some fine players but by the mid-1930s a promising start almost ended in relegation. In 1936 the strain of managing the club on and off the field began to take its toll and, after a dangerous illness, Patterson gave up his managerial role although he continued as club secretary. It was clearly a wise decision and Patterson lived on until 1955.

PAYNE, JIMMY. Outside-right who played in Liverpool's post-war teams. Although Payne came to Anfield during the mid-1940s he did not make his league debut until 1948, at the age of 22. He was a member of Liverpool's losing FA Cup final side in 1950 and chalked up almost 250 games for the Reds, scoring 42 goals. He was said to be a useful little winger and even won an England B cap but with players like Matthews and Finney around there was little hope of him ever winning a full England cap. In April 1956 he was surprisingly sold to Everton but had only six outings with the Goodison club before retiring.

PEAKE, ERNEST. Welsh international centre-half who made 51 league appearances for Liverpool prior to the First World War. Peake came to Anfield in 1908, making his debut a year later but left to join Third Lanark in 1914. He was capped ten times by Wales while he was at Liverpool.

PENALTY SHOOT-OUTS. Liverpool have been involved in two memorable penalty shoot-outs. The first came at the end of extra-time in the 1984 European Cup final against Roma. After Steve Nicol had missed the first kick, Liverpool eventually won the game when Alan Kennedy slammed his attempt firmly into the back of the net. The second exciting shoot-out came in the replay of the 1992 FA Cup semi-final against Portsmouth. This time Liverpool's win was more convincing.

PEPLOW, STEVE. Just three appearances for Liverpool, two of them in the league and the other in Europe against Vitoria Setubal of Portugal. Peplow will be best remembered on Merseyside for his many outings with Tranmere Rovers. He came to Liverpool as an apprentice in 1966 but having failed to make the grade he eventually wound up at Prenton Park after various periods with Swindon, Nottingham Forest and Mansfield. He played well over 200 games for Tranmere.

PERKINS, BILL. Liverpool goalkeeper as the club captured its first ever league championship in 1901. Tall, strong and dependable, Perkins was signed in 1898 from Luton Town. He made 107 league appearances for Liverpool before moving to Northampton Town in 1903.

PIECHNIK, TORBEN. Danish international defender, signed in 1992 from the Danish club Bk 1903. Piechnik was a member of the Danish international squad that lifted the 1992 European championships and starred in the final as Denmark beat Germany 2–0. After a hesitant start with Liverpool he built up a steady partnership with Steve Nicol at the centre of defence. Tall, athletic and quick off the mark, Piechnik was a bargain buy at a time when exorbitant prices were being demanded for second-rate English defenders. But it never really worked out for him at Anfield and in 1994 he returned to Denmark.

PITCH. The Anfield pitch measures 110 yards×75 yards.

PRATT, DAVID. Former Celtic defender who came to Liverpool via Bradford City in November 1921. He went on to play 77 league games before moving on to Bury in 1927. Later he had a successful career in management with Notts County, Hearts and Port Vale.

PRIDAY, BOB. South African winger with 33 appearances during the years after the Second World War. He was an able deputy to Billy Liddell but was not a member of the championship-winning side of 1947–48. He was transferred to Blackburn Rovers in 1949.

PROGRAMME. The Liverpool programme began life as a joint effort with Everton Football Club. It was produced each week with the line-ups for the first team game as well as for their neighbour's reserve match being played at the other ground. The two clubs continued to share the programme for almost 50 years until 1934 when they went their separate ways. Since then it has developed from the cheap and bland few pages of the 1950s to the rather more expensive glossy, colour production of today.

PROMOTION. Liverpool have been promoted on four occasions and always from the second division to the first. They were first promoted in 1894 when they won the second division title and the subsequent play-offs. Two years later they were again promoted when they topped the second division and won the play-offs. In 1905 they were promoted for the third time and again as champions. They were last promoted in 1962, as second division champions for the fourth time. Liverpool are only one of a handful of clubs who have won the second and first division championship in consecutive years, winning the second division title in 1905 and the first division a year later.

PURSELL, BOB. Liverpool full-back who was banned from

football following the infamous fixed match against Manchester United in 1915. Pursell had joined Liverpool from the famous Scottish club Queen's Park in September 1911. Unfortunately, in their eagerness to sign Pursell, Liverpool overlooked one or two legal niceties and were subsequently fined £250 for failing to talk with Queen's Park in the first place. Pursell made 112 appearances for Liverpool until his suspension which was lifted after the war, by which time he had joined Port Vale.

Q

QUICKEST GOAL. Timings of goals are notoriously unreliable, particularly as you go back to earlier years, but the 1928–29 season offers a few contenders for the prize. And it was certainly a season when turning up late would have meant missing the goals. Liverpool kicked off their season at Anfield with the new Kop being opened and within a minute were a goal up against Bury. Six weeks later Dick Edmed scored first-minute goals, home and away, in consecutive weeks and then in November Gordon Hodgson struck almost from the start to give Liverpool the lead against Bolton Wanderers at Anfield.

R

RAISBECK, ALEX. One of the great names in the history of Liverpool Football Club, Raisbeck was a distinguished centre-half who dominated life at Anfield in the days before the First World War. He joined Liverpool from Stoke in May 1898, having earlier played with Hibernian, and went on to play 340 games for Liverpool before joining Partick Thistle in 1909. During those years he helped Liverpool to two league championships as well as the second division title and was capped eight times by his country. Raisbeck was an enormous power at Anfield and has to go down as the first of a number of outstanding Scots who would influence the course of the club's history over the next century. Strong, athletic and a great leader, Raisbeck skippered the club for many years. After Partick Thistle he joined Hamilton Academicals and later managed Bristol City, Halifax and Chester. He returned to Anfield shortly before the Second World War to take on a scouting job. He died in a Liverpool hospital in March 1949.

RAMSDEN, BERNIE. Left-back with 66 appearances to his credit between 1937 and 1948. He made 23 appearances for Liverpool's post-war championship side, continuing his wartime link with Jim Harley, but by then Ramsden was already 30 and was beginning to suffer from injury. The war years had robbed him of what might have been a glittering career and in 1948 his Liverpool career drew to a close when he was transferred to Sunderland. He had joined Liverpool in 1935 from Sheffield Victoria.

RAWLINGS, ARCHIE. Winger Archie Rawlings was already an England international when he arrived at Anfield from Preston North End in 1924. Capped in 1921 as England faced the Olympic champions Belgium, Rawlings had an appalling debut in England's 2–0 win and was never capped again. By the time he arrived at Anfield he was already the wrong side of 30. He stayed for just two years, making 67 appearances and scoring ten goals, then moved on to Walsall and later had outings with Bradford Park Avenue and Southport.

RAYBOULD, SAM. One of the finest goalscorers in the club's history. In 224 games Raybould netted an astonishing 127 goals. His best figures were in the 1902–03 season when he scored 31 league goals in 33 matches. It was to be a record that would stand until Gordon Hodgson netted 36 goals in a season, 29 years later. Raybould joined Liverpool in 1900 from New Brighton Tower, having had previous spells with Derby County and Chesterfield. Over the next eight seasons he steered Liverpool to two league titles and the second division championship. Strangely, however, he was never capped by England although he did play for the Football League against the Scottish League on three occasions. In 1907 he joined Sunderland and a year later was transferred to Arsenal.

REAKES, SIDNEY. Former Liverpool chairman and director. Joined the Liverpool board in 1955 and succeeded T. V. Williams as chairman in 1964. He was for many years the club's longest serving director, until his sudden death in November 1992.

RECORDS. Liverpool have beaten plenty of records over the years but one of the least mentioned was a long-playing record released in early 1972 and called *The Kop Choir*. It featured all the Kop favourites and was produced by Watney Mann and CBS records. Liverpool have produced a number of discs since then but alas none have gone on to top the charts in quite the same way as their exploits on the football field.

REDKNAPP, JAMIE. Signed from Bournemouth by Kenny Dalglish for a fee of £350,000. The son of the then Bournemouth manager Harry Redknapp, Jamie was only 17 when he joined Liverpool but had already shown enormous potential. Within a year of his arrival he was given his chance and has since gone on to prove a valuable acquisition. A tall, powerful midfielder who likes to go forward, he scored his first goal for Liverpool in the final minute of a league match at Anfield against Chelsea in September 1992, a goal, appropriately at the Kop end, which gave Liverpool a much needed victory. Since then Redknapp has gone from strength to strength winning international honours at Under-21 and full level. He also won a winners medal in the Coca-Cola Cup in 1995.

REFEREES. At least one Liverpool player has turned his hand to refereeing at the end of his playing days. But the most noteworthy of them has to be Matt McQueen, the one-time Liverpool captain. McQueen, who later went on to become a director of the club and then manager between 1923 and 1928, was also a Football League referee, qualifying after his playing career came to an end in 1900.

REID, TOM. Although Tom Reid played more than 50 games for Liverpool he found greater fame with Manchester United. It was surprising that Liverpool should have let him go, especially as he had scored 31 goals in 51 league appearances. They were impressive figures and they con-

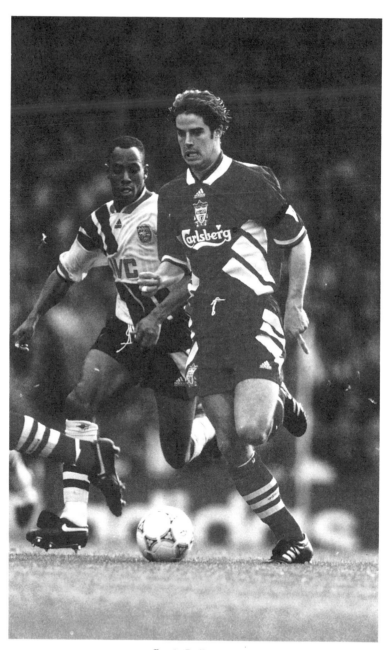

Jamie Redknapp

tinued at Old Trafford with Reid knocking in 67 goals in 107 outings, though they were still not enough to stop United avoiding the drop into division two. Eighteen months later he was on the move again, this time to Oldham, where his prolific goalscoring continued un-abated. Reid had come to Liverpool in 1926, a £1,000 signing from Clydebank, and left in 1929.

RELEGATION. Liverpool have been relegated on only three occasions. Their first taste came in 1895 after just one season in the first division. Fortunately they were promoted the following season. They were next relegated in 1904 but again returned to the first division the following season and then promptly won the first division championship. Liverpool's third experience of relegation came in 1954. This time it took them eight seasons to escape the second division.

RILEY, ARTHUR. South African goalkeeper of the inter-war years. Along with Gordon Hodgson he caught Liverpool's eye during the South Africans' soccer tour of 1924. Riley was signed immediately, with Hodgson arriving four months later. But the job Riley faced at Anfield was enormous; he was expected to take over from the legendary Elisha Scott. It was, of course, an impossible task yet he carried it out with much distinction and served Liverpool well during most of the 1930s, playing 338 games during a period when Liverpool could best be described as a mid-table side. He left Merseyside and returned to South Africa with the outbreak of war.

ROBERTSON, JOHN. Right-back John Robertson had already enjoyed something of a glittering career by the time he signed for Liverpool. A star with Hibernian, he had also played for Stoke and joined Liverpool in 1900. He stayed for just two years but it was enough to win him a league championship medal in 1901. He looked set for a long career at Anfield but, for one reason or another, he decided that he wanted away. Liverpool were deeply upset but could not persuade the man from joining Southampton where he helped them to two Southern League championships. He made 46 appearances for Liverpool.

ROBERTSON, TOMMY. Scottish international winger signed from Scottish champions Heart of Midlothian in 1898. Robertson played 126 games, scoring 34 goals over five seasons before returning to Hearts. He was a member of Liverpool's first championship side.

ROBINSON, MICHAEL. The signing of Michael Robinson during the summer of 1983 surprised many supporters. Robinson had been labelled a 'golden boy' when Manchester City paid Preston a staggering £750,000 for his services in 1979. But he never quite seemed to make the grade at Maine Road and a year later he was sold to Brighton for half the price. It was claimed that Liverpool had long admired him and at £200,000 it seemed worth the risk. A little over a year later he was sold to Queen's Park Rangers, the fee halved yet again. Robinson had made just 26 league appearances, scoring six goals, and had never looked to have the flair or dash of a Liverpool forward. He later played for Osasuna in the Spanish League. He was capped 23 times by the Republic of Ireland and now enjoys a successful career with Spanish television as a commentator.

ROBINSON, PETER. Liverpool secretary since June 1965. Peter Robinson's travels have taken him from Stockport to Crewe to Scunthorpe to Brighton and finally to Anfield where he has now become part of the fixtures and fittings. Highly respected throughout the game, he began as a 17-year-old office boy at Stockport County. When he left five years later he was assistant secretary. He then became secretary at Crewe, Scunthorpe and Brighton. Once described by former chairman Sir John Smith as 'one of the best signings we ever made', Robinson's wise counsel has contributed as much as anything to Liverpool's phenomenal success over the years. He was appointed a director of the club in 1993.

ROBINSON, ROBBIE. Liverpool manager Tom Watson returned to his old stomping ground at Sunderland to make one of his most valuable acquisitions in Robert Robinson. He was signed in 1904 after just a few outings with the north-east club but went on to make well over 250 appearances in a red shirt over the next eight years. Powerful and adept, Robinson won league championship honours and division two honours with Liverpool before joining Tranmere Rovers in 1912.

ROME. Scene of two great Liverpool triumphs. Their first appearance in Rome came in the 1977 European Cup final when they beat Borussia Moenchengladbach 3–1 to win their first European Cup. Their second triumph in the Eternal City came in 1984 when they beat AS Roma on their own ground, the Olympic Stadium, to win the European Cup for a fourth time.

ROSENTHAL, RONNY. Israeli international who burst on to the Anfield scene to help steer Liverpool to the league title in 1990. Rosenthal initially came to Liverpool on an extended loan after a number of clubs, including Luton, had decided to dispense with him after trying him out. Rosenthal was immediately effective at Anfield, adding an extra dimension to the Liverpool attack just when it was most needed. He seemed to have the ability to hold the ball as he barged his way into the area, with defenders having no end of trouble in dispossessing him. Joining Liverpool towards the end of the 1989–90 season, his goals and efforts provided the extra fillip Liverpool needed to clinch the title. At the end of the season Liverpool decided to sign him permanently, paying the Belgian club Standard Liege £500,000. Since then, however, he has never been quite as effective and his appearances have been limited, usually as a substitute. His previous clubs included Maccabi and FC Bruges as well as Standard Liege. Joined Tottenham in 1994 for £250,000.

ROSS, IAN. Amiable Glaswegian who grew up with Kenny Dalglish but who did not share quite the same degree of success as the latter. Ross could play anywhere and although he enjoyed his days at Anfield he was never a regular. His best season was probably his last, 1971–72, when he made 20 league appearances. But over six seasons he only managed a total of 59 games. His finest moment came against Bayern Munich in the UEFA Cup when Bill Shankly asked him to mark Franz Beckenbauer, a daunting task if ever there was one. Yet Ross performed magnificently, snuffing the German captain out of the game altogether. In 1972 he was transferred to Aston Villa for £60,000 and he helped them to the third division title and the Football League Cup. He later played with Notts County, Northampton, Peterborough and Wolves. Subsequently he became a manager and enjoyed a spell with Huddersfield Town.

ROSS, JIMMY. One of the outstanding names of nineteenth-century soccer, Jimmy Ross came from a renowned footballing family, his brother Nick having been a star with Everton and Preston North End. The two brothers spent most of their careers with Preston, playing in the great Invincibles' side that won so many honours. Jimmy himself picked up two league championship medals and an FA Cup winners' medal as well as a losers' medal. Honours continued to come his way at Anfield where he picked up a second division winners' medal. He also won a similar honour with Burnley two years later. Ross was actually born in Edinburgh, coming to Preston North End in 1884. He once scored eight goals in a game as Preston thrashed Hyde 26–0 in the FA Cup. Ross was a great capture for Liverpool yet he almost never came. Having agreed to sign for the club, his brother Nick was taken seriously ill and on his death bed pleaded with Jimmy to remain with Preston. Jimmy was torn but in the end decided that he had to keep his agreement with Liverpool. At the time he cost Liverpool £75, the biggest fee they had ever paid for a player. He went on to play 78 league games for Liverpool and even skippered the side for some time. In 1894 he left Liverpool for Burnley, helping them into the first division, and then joined Manchester City where he played alongside the great Billy Meredith. He died in 1902 while still on City's books. Neither he nor his brother were ever capped by their country as the Scottish FA refused at that time to choose players who had deserted their shores.

ROWLEY, TONY. Perhaps best remembered as a Tranmere Rovers player, Rowley began his league career at Anfield. Born in the Midlands, he was originally on Birmingham City's books but failed to make any league appearances and was transferred to non-league Stourbridge. Liverpool picked him up in October 1953. He scored a hat trick on his debut and his tally of 38 goals in 61 appearances over four seasons is quite impressive. But Rowley had his critics. He was said to be slow, to lack class and consequently drifted in and out of the team. Perhaps under a more positive manager he might have proved his worth. As it was, Tranmere signed him in 1958 for £3,500 and he went on to score 51 goals in 108 outings.

ROYALTY. Liverpool were involved in a piece of royal history when King George V became the first ever reigning monarch to watch a Cup final: he saw Liverpool play Burnley at the Crystal Palace in 1914. The first royal visitors to Anfield were King George V and Queen Mary, who watched the 1921 FA Cup semi-final between Wolves and Cardiff. The previous March the King had watched Liverpool playing Manchester City at their Hyde Road ground in Manchester. Anfield had to wait some time for its next royal visitor, until March 1973, when the Duke of Kent visited the club and officially opened the new Main Stand.

After Hillsborough there were further visits, with Prince Charles representing the royal family. In 1993 Her Majesty the Queen also toured Anfield, meeting the players and staff and visiting the Hillsborough memorial.

RUDDOCK, NEIL. Defender signed from Tottenham Hotspur in July 1993 for a fee of £2.5m. He previously played for Millwall and Southampton. Ruddock's career at Anfield, however, did not begin comfortably. For some time he looked hopelessly out of place in the centre of defence and there was much talk about him being sold. But after the departure of Souness he seemed to regain confidence and during the 1994–95 season was one of the side's undoubted successes. Indeed he was so successful that he ended the season playing for England and with a winners' medal from the Coca-Cola Cup. Now a great favourite with the fans.

RUDHAM, DOUG. Another South African goalkeeper who joined Liverpool in 1954. Like Arthur Riley earlier, he too was spotted while touring with the 1954 South African national side. He went on to make 63 league appearances before returning to South Africa in 1960.

RUMBELOWS CUP. See **FOOTBALL LEAGUE CUP.**

RUNNERS-UP. Liverpool have been first division runners-up on ten occasions. When this is added to their 18 championship titles it means that the club has finished in the top two for 28 years of its 100-year history.

RUSH, IAN. The finest marksman in the club's history. Born in St Asaph in 1961, Rush was initially snapped up by Chester. After only a handful of league appearances he had a glut of first division clubs queuing up for his signature. Favourites to sign him were Manchester City, but they baulked at the £300,000 asking price and thereby missed out on the most prolific goalscorer of the 1980s. Liverpool had no such hesitations. He made his debut in December

Ian Rush

1980 but in seven outings failed to score. It was not until October 1981 that he finally began to secure his place although even then the goals were still slow in arriving. Paisley's advice to the young man was simple: be more selfish in front of goal. It seemed to do the trick, and by the end of that season he had netted 17 goals in 32 league appearances. It was the beginning of the Rush years and his partnership with Kenny Dalglish proved to be one of the most exciting Anfield had ever seen. League championships, FA Cups, European Cups and honours galore flooded into Anfield and always it was Rush slamming in the vital goals. His best season was 1983–84 when he struck 48 goals in 64 games. His pace was phenomenal, his sharpness in front of goal devastating, and he could leave defenders standing with his speed. It was Rush who turned a lacklustre performance against Everton in the 1986 FA Cup final into a memorable occasion as he snatched a couple of goals to present Liverpool with the Double. He even managed five goals in one league match and went on to beat the great Dixie Dean's goalscoring record in derbies. It was inevitable that some foreign club would lure him away and in June 1987 he duly signed for Juventus in a record-breaking £3 million deal. But his days in Italy were marred by illness, a car crash, and an inability to escape the tight marking of Italian defences. Juventus had also recently lost their playmakers, Platini and Boniek, with Rush never given the kind of support up front that he needed. The result was a disappointment and at the end of the season Juventus were ready to let him return to Anfield. It took him a while to regain his sharpness and as the years have gone on Rush has developed a new role for himself. Always a hard worker and a runner, Rush has continued to make an impact. Although the goals have never been as regular as they once were, he has continued to terrify defences throughout the Football League. Capped by Wales on more than 57 occasions, he is also the top goalscorer for his country. During the 1992–93 season Rush broke Roger Hunt's record haul of 286 goals for the club with his first ever goal against Manchester

United and his first in the Premier League. Has played more than 600 games for Liverpool and has scored over 330 goals.

S

SANDON HOTEL. The public house in Oakfield Road, close to Anfield, owned by John Houlding. For some years it was the headquarters of Everton Football Club before the rift that led to the formation of Liverpool FC. It was often used as a changing place for the players before they made their way to Anfield and for many years was a focal point for Liverpool supporters before and after matches.

SAUNDERS, DEAN. Became the most expensive player in Britain when Liverpool signed him from Derby County for £2.9 million during the 1991 close season. Much was expected of Saunders, who had been a spectacular goal-scorer with Oxford United and Derby, but sadly he never really showed the same sharpness at Anfield. Perhaps he was overawed by his new surroundings or simply did not wear the tag of Britain's costliest player too comfortably. Unfortunately he also came into a Liverpool side under-going radical change and hit by injury. John Barnes was missing and Saunders never received the kind of service he needed, as Liverpool continued to play a very different game to the one that Saunders excelled in. In September 1992 he was sold to Aston Villa for £2.3 million and his career was suddenly resurrected. Saunders, the son of the former Liverpool half-back Roy Saunders, did, however, claim one Anfield record by being the first Liverpool player ever to score four goals in a European game, when Liverpool beat Kuusysi Lahti 6–1 at Anfield. In five European appearances Saunders netted nine goals. His league scoring record, however, left much to be desired, just 11 goals in 42 games during the 1991–92 season. Saunders was also a Welsh international, capped more than 40 times by his country. His career began where his father's career had left off, at Swansea, who allowed him to join Brighton on a free transfer. He later went to Oxford United and was involved in a £1 million transfer to Derby that resulted in the sacking of Oxford manager and former Red favourite Mark Lawrenson, who had complained bitterly to the Maxwells about the sale of the young man.

SAUNDERS, ROY. Father of Dean Saunders. Right-half of the 1950s who began his Anfield playing career as Liverpool slipped from the first to the second division. Consequently, the vast majority of his appearances were in the second division as Liverpool struggled to regain a foothold in the higher league. Unfortunately they did not make it during his time and in March 1959 he was sold to Swansea. A former England youth international, his opportunities at Anfield were limited by the presence of Bob Paisley and Phil Taylor.

SAUNDERS, TOM. Member of the Liverpool backroom staff for many years. A Liverpool schoolteacher, Tom Saunders was the manager of the Liverpool Boys side from 1958 to 1970. From 1960 to 1970 he was also coach and then manager of the England schoolboy team. In 1970 he quit his job as a headmaster to become Youth Development Officer at Anfield and in that capacity has overseen the progress of most of the youngsters on the Liverpool staff. Since then he has also travelled the world on spying missions for the club, producing dossiers on teams and players that were to be crucial in Liverpool's European successes. He has also managed the England Under-18 side. He retired in 1986 but was appointed a director in 1993.

SAWYER, ERIC. Liverpool director for many years. He became a director of the club during the early 1960s and headed the finance committee, providing the money for many transfer deals. Along with chairman T. V. Williams, Eric Sawyer was the board member most responsible for turning Anfield into a modern stadium and supplying a ready flow of cash for the manager to build one of the strongest teams in Europe. He died in May 1979.

SCALES, JOHN. A £3.5 million signing from Wimbledon in September 1994. Having just signed Phil Babb from Coventry for a similar fee, the signing of John Scales a few days later came as something of a surprise, especially as both men seemed to fill the same position. Scales, however, has proved to be more than value for his huge fee, fitting into the back line as if he had been a Liverpool player all his life. Joined Wimbledon from Bristol Rovers and then spent seven years with the South London club, converting from full-back to centre half. He had begun his career with Leeds United but was clearly not part of their plans and was transferred to Bristol Rovers. His impressive start at Anfield ended with England honours and a winners' medal in the Coca-Cola Cup. Scales is in the tradition of Liverpool central defenders – tall, elegant and calm, always looking to play the ball out of defence.

SCANDAL. The biggest scandal in Liverpool's history came on Good Friday 1915 when a game between Liverpool and Manchester United was fixed beforehand. United, facing relegation, were desperate for points, whereas Liverpool, in mid-table, had little to play for. But the real motive was to make money out of a betting coup. Bets were placed by some of the players, throughout the country, on a score of 2–0 for United. And that was precisely how the game turned out. Not all the players were in on the deal but, from the way the game was being played, it was apparent not only to the players but also to the spectators that something was going on. An FA inquiry later resulted in the suspension of eight players. The Liverpool culprits were Jackie Sheldon, a former United player who was reckoned to be the instigator, Bob Pursell, Tommy Miller and Tom Fairfoul. All were suspended until after the war.

SCORES – HIGHEST. Liverpool's highest score in any game was their 11–0 win over Stromgodset in the European Cup Winners Cup on 17 September 1974. The club's best ever victory in the Football League was a 10–1 win over Rotherham Town in the second division on 18 February 1896.

SCOTLAND. Liverpool have always had close links with Scottish football. Their first ever team, known as the 'team of the all Macs', was composed almost entirely of Scots, and over the years players like Raisbeck, Liddell, Dalglish, Souness and Hansen along with manager Bill Shankly have had a dramatic influence on the club's fortunes. Kenny Dalglish remains the most capped Scottish player in Liverpool's history, winning a total of 55 caps during his years at Anfield.

SCOTT, ELISHA. Perhaps the finest goalkeeper ever to serve on Liverpool books and one of the greatest of all time. Elisha Scott, the brother of Billy Scott, the Everton goalkeeper, initially went to Everton for a trial but the Goodison club reckoned he was too small as well as too young. Brother Billy had a word with John McKenna at Anfield. McKenna and Tom Watson came to see him play and, although he was only 17, had no hesitations about signing him on the spot. Fortunately Scott soon sprouted a few inches, although he never went beyond 5ft 9in. His early chances at Anfield were severely limited by the presence of Kenny Campbell but just as the First World

Elisha Scott

War broke out Scott finally secured the 'keeper's jersey and afterwards was the regular choice until 1934. In all he played 18 seasons for Liverpool, making 467 appearances, and would most certainly have played well over 500 games but for the First World War. Scott was majestic: slim, agile and dedicated to the art of goalkeeping, he soon became a great favourite of the Kop. During the late 1920s his tussles with Everton's Dixie Dean were legendary. It was once said that when they met in a Liverpool street Dean politely nodded to him and Scott leapt to the ground to save some imaginary header. At the beginning of his career Newcastle tried to sign him, even offering £1,000, and although Scott was eager to move the Liverpool manager, Tom Watson, would hear none of it. Then in 1934 Everton, no doubt weary of his exploits and somewhat embarrassed by their earlier mistake, made an audacious bid to take him across Stanley Park. At first it seemed they might be successful but as the letters poured into the *Liverpool Echo*, Liverpool backed away from any thoughts of doing a deal with Everton. At the end of that season, however, Scott decided to try his luck back home and moved to Ireland as manager of Belfast Celtic. Scott was capped 31 times by Northern Ireland, winning his first cap in 1920 and his last in 1936 while he was with Belfast Celtic. Twenty-seven of his caps were won while he was with Liverpool.

SCREEN SPORT SUPER CUP. Sometimes known simply as the Super Cup. The cup was contested just once, during the 1985–86 season between the six teams who would have qualified for Europe. In the final, which took place the following season, Liverpool faced Everton in a two-legged match. Liverpool won the first leg at Anfield 3–1 and the second leg at Goodison by 4–1 to take the trophy 7–2 on aggregate.

SECOND DIVISON. Liverpool have had four spells in the second division. The first was their initial league season, 1893–94. At the end of that season they topped the table, not having lost a single game, and were duly promoted after the play-offs. Unfortunately they survived only one season in the top division before sliding back into the second. But again it was just for one season, 1895–96, and at the end of the campaign they were once more topping the table. Again they won promotion after the play-offs. Their third experience of second division soccer came during the

1904–5 season, but as on the previous occasions it lasted just one season. Liverpool's last taste of the lower division began in 1954 but this time lasted eight seasons before they topped the table in 1962. On each of the four occasions that Liverpool have been promoted they have topped the table.

SEMI-FINALS. Up to the end of the 1992–93 season Liverpool had been involved in 19 FA Cup semi-finals.

SHANKLY, BILL. Liverpool manager, 1959 to 1974. Shankly is probably the most legendary figure in the history of Liverpool Football Club and the driving force that was to turn a second division side with a proud history into one of the most famous clubs in world soccer. He was born in Glenbuck in Lanarkshire on 2 September 1913, one of ten children. Shankly's footballing career began south of the border with Carlisle United, where he made his league debut during the 1932–33 season. After just 16 appearances Preston North End signed the youngster for £500 and over the next 16 years he went on to make 300 appearances for the Deepdale club, though war robbed him of many more games. A strong, refined wing-half, Shankly was also capped five times by his country. In March 1949 he was offered his first chance in management at his former club Carlisle. He remained there just two years before Grimsby Town, then in the third division north, tempted him with another managerial post. That job lasted almost four years before he surprisingly quit to join struggling Workington Town. A year later he was on the move again, this time as assistant manager to Andy Beattie at first division Huddersfield Town. Within the year, however, Huddersfield had been relegated and Beattie sacked. It was unfortunate for Huddersfield but lucky for Shankly who was immediately appointed manager, a post which lasted for three years before Liverpool, then in the second division, stepped in with an offer. When he arrived at Anfield in December 1959 he was shocked at the state of the club and

Bill Shankly

immediately began a rebuilding programme. Most of the players he inherited were transferred, new players were bought and even the club's training ground at Melwood was refurbished. Shankly's first masterstroke was to sign Ron Yeats and Ian St John, who over the next decade formed the backbone of his side. Others such as Gordon Milne, Peter Thompson and Willie Stevenson were among his early signings while chances were given to youngsters such as Chris Lawler, Gerry Byrne, Tommy Smith and Roger Hunt. Shankly's first success came in 1962 as Liverpool lifted the second division championship. Two years later they were league champions and followed that up in 1965 by winning the FA Cup for the first time in their history.

Over the next nine years, as Shankly ruled supreme at Anfield, Liverpool lifted two more league titles as well as the FA Cup for a second time and the UEFA Cup. In 1974, following their FA Cup victory, Shankly shocked the footballing world by sensationally resigning. There had been no hint of it although he had often threatened to resign over matters of principle in the past. This time he claimed he was tired and in need of a rest. But it was not long before he missed the game and he was soon taking on various consultancy roles. Sadly, he was never offered any other post at Anfield, nor even a directorship, and in his later years he felt bitter about the way the club had treated him. He died on 29 September 1981, a few days after suffering a heart attack. Without a doubt Shankly was one of the great managers of the modern era – fanatical, loyal and always ready with a quip. He once said that he and Liverpool Football Club were made for each other. It was undoubtedly true. Shankly created the modern Liverpool, turning a sleeping giant into the great club it is today. It was Shankly who laid down the ground rules, who created the bootroom, the development of talent in the reserves, the passing game that was to become Liverpool's hallmark and the commitment to the club that was demanded of every player. They were rules which were to serve Liverpool well over the next 20 years.

SHANKLY GATES. The Shankly Gates were erected as a permanent memorial to Bill Shankly with the sign 'You'll Never Walk Alone' above them. They were formally opened by his widow Nessie Shankly.

SHEEDY, KEVIN. Even Liverpool can make mistakes. For a number of seasons reserve midfielder Kevin Sheedy stood on the brink of an Anfield career but with Graeme Souness ahead of him the chances were few and far between. He made just one full appearance for the Reds – his debut was in February 1981 – and a year later was sold to Everton for £100,000. It turned out to be a bargain. Before long the

The Shankly Gates

Liverpool midfield was crying out for him. Sheedy went on to have a glittering career across Stanley Park and was a major influence on the Everton side that won two league titles in the mid-1980s.

SHELDON, JACKIE. The former Manchester United right-winger John Sheldon was the man said to be behind the 1915 betting scandal that rocked English football. Sheldon was rumoured to have acted as go-between when Liverpool and Manchester United players fixed the result of their Good Friday 1915 meeting. Along with others Sheldon was suspended but following the war his suspension was lifted. He joined Liverpool from United in November 1913. After 129 outings, injury forced his retirement in 1922. At United he had been understudy to the great Billy Meredith.

SHONE, DANNY. Centre-forward in the 1922 league championship side. Signed as a replacement for the injured Dick Johnson, Shone more than played his part as Liverpool stormed to the title, netting six league goals in 15 appearances. But when Johnson returned to fitness, Shone

189

lost his place the following season. His subsequent Anfield appearances were limited, though he did make 42 appearances in the 1924–25 season. He was transferred to West Ham in 1928 and later played with Coventry.

SIDLOW, CYRIL. Liverpool goalkeeper during the post-war years. He made 165 appearances for the club between 1946 and 1951, winning a league championship medal and an FA Cup runners-up medal as well as seven Welsh caps. Sidlow was signed for a record fee for a goalkeeper of £5,000 from Wolverhampton Wanderers in 1946 where he had already won 11 wartime caps. He went on to become a great favourite with the Anfield crowd. At times he could be inconsistent but he will always be remembered as one of the first goalkeepers to regularly throw the ball out of his area rather than simply kick it upfield. In August 1952 he joined New Brighton.

SLATER, BERT. Scottish-born goalkeeper Slater was involved in a surprise exchange transfer that took Anfield favourite Tommy Younger back to Scotland and Falkirk. But Slater was never as good as Younger and three years later was sold to Dundee, although in between he had won a second division championship medal. Slater won Scotland Under-23 honours and also a Scottish Cup winners' medal during his days at Falkirk. He later won a Scottish Cup runners-up medal with Dundee.

SMALLEST PLAYER. Although such statistics are always unreliable and were generally not even available for those playing before 1900, the distinction of being Liverpool's smallest player probably has to be shared by three men. They were Mervyn Jones, an outside-left in the early 1950s who played just four games for the club; James McBride, a left-half with 30 league outings during the club's formative years; and Robert Neil, a Scot who had 23 games, astonishingly, as a centre-half during the 1896–97 season. All three men stood at 5ft 4ins.

SMITH, JIM. While everybody knows the name of Dixie Dean, very few remember Jim Smith. Yet Smith holds the record as the highest goalscorer in British football, having netted 66 league goals for Ayr United as they won the 1928 Scottish second division. Interestingly, it was the same season as Dean smashed the Football League record. Smith immediately became one of the hottest properties in the game and a year later joined Liverpool for what was then a British record fee of £5,500. For a few seasons the two leading goalscorers in British history were both playing in the city of Liverpool. Smith, however, never quite had the touch of Dean, although he did score 38 goals in his 61 league appearances for Liverpool. He was eventually transferred to Tunbridge Wells in July 1932 and later played with Bristol Rovers, Newport County and Notts County before joining Dumbarton as player-manager.

SMITH, SIR JOHN. Liverpool chairman during most of the years of the club's phenomenal success. Smith was appointed chairman of Liverpool in 1973 after having served for many years as a director of the club. In 1985 he was also appointed chairman of the Sports Council. Smith was very much the inspiration behind Kenny Dalglish's appointment as manager and his professional approach to his job won him praise throughout football. He retired as chairman of the club in 1990 and continued to serve as a director until his death in 1995.

SMITH, TOMMY. One of the Anfield immortals whose greatest moment came in what was supposed to be his last game for the club. Playing in the 1977 European Cup final, Smith appeared from out of nowhere to head Liverpool into a unassailable 2–1 lead. It was possibly the most important goal in the club's history and more than fitting that Smith should have been the man to score it. Carried away by his moment of glory, Smith decided to have another season at Anfield. He finally left the club at the end of that season, joining his former Anfield colleague John

191

Tommy Smith

Toshack at Swansea. Liverpudlian Smith had joined Anfield as a teenager, making his league debut in the 5–1 victory over Birmingham City in May 1963 when he was just 18 years and one month old. In his early days he was regarded as an inside-left but he soon became renowned as the toughest defender in the game. He was uncompromising; quick in the tackle and fearless, yet he had far more skill than was ever accorded him. In 15 seasons in the top flight at Anfield he played 632 games but won just one England cap. Yet he more than made up for his lack of England honours by a glut of medals at club level – four league championship medals, two FA Cup, two UEFA Cup and a European Cup winners' medal plus a bagful of runners-up medals. Few players in the history of the club have been as popular as Smith, who came to epitomise the 'never-say-die' spirit of Anfield. After Swansea he had a brief spell back at Anfield as a coach.

SOUNESS, GRAEME. Player and manager. Although he

was born in Edinburgh, Graeme Souness's footballing career began south of the border with Tottenham Hotspur. But it was not a particularly memorable time, his only appearance coming as a substitute in European competition. At one point he even ran away from London, back home to Edinburgh, though he was eventually persuaded back to Tottenham. His differences with the club continued and in January 1973 Spurs sold the young man to Middlesbrough where, under manager Jack Charlton, his career finally began to blossom: there he won a second division championship medal. Five years later, in January 1978, Bob Paisley paid £325,000 to bring him to Anfield in what was to prove one of the club's best ever signings. Over the next six years Souness would inspire Liverpool to triumphs across Europe and at home. In all he collected three European Cup winners' medals, five league championship medals and four Football League Cup medals. He was also capped 54 times by his country, with the vast majority coming while he was at Anfield. Souness was as authoritative a midfielder as any in the club's long history. He was a general, controlling the centre of the park with a swagger and determination that won him both admirers and enemies. He was to go down as one of the club's finest ever captains. Quick to the tackle, unflinching, as well as creative, Souness was unquestionably one of the greatest midfielders British football has seen, oozing determination and commitment. After six successful years at Anfield he decided to see out his final days in Italy, signing for Sampdoria for £650,000 in June 1984. Two years later he made a surprise return to British football, joining Glasgow Rangers as player-manager. Yet despite Souness being sent off in his first match, within a year the Glasgow club were Scottish league champions. Suddenly Ibrox was alight, the stadium filled to capacity most Saturdays, as Souness revolutionised the Scottish transfer market by tempting numerous English stars north of the border. They included Terry Butcher, Chris Woods, Mark Hateley, Mark Walters, Trevor Francis, Ray Wilkins and Nigel Spackman. His

Graeme Souness

tactics paid handsome dividends as the club went on to win even more honours. Souness was even appointed a director of Rangers. The resignation of Kenny Dalglish, however, almost inevitably meant that Souness would wind up back at Anfield, and towards the end of the 1990–91 season he was forced to admit to a stunned Glasgow that he was indeed Liverpool-bound. Souness's arrival at Anfield initiated major changes. Players such as Peter Beardsley, Barry Venison, Gary Ablett, Glenn Hysen, Steve McMahon, Steve Staunton, Gary Gillespie and Ray Houghton were sold as part of a policy of introducing youth. New players were bought – Dean Saunders, Mark Wright, Mark Walters, Paul Stewart, Michael Thomas, Rob Jones, plus the Scandanavians Stig Bjornebye and Torben Piechnik – while some of Anfield's youngsters were given their chance. It was a massive turnaround of playing staff that did not really help continuity. At the same time there were serious long-term injuries affecting a number of players, including John Barnes, Ronnie Whelan and Jan Molby, that again did little to help matters. In his first full season in charge results went from bad to worse and Liverpool were never really title contenders. In the end they finished up in sixth place, their worst position since 1965. But if results did not go well in the league, Souness could certainly claim some satisfaction in the FA Cup as Liverpool went on to win the trophy, beating Sunderland 2–0 in the final. The following season, 1992–93, turned out to be even worse than the previous season with further injuries and poor form at one stage plunging Liverpool into the relegation zone. By January they were out of every competition, even beaten at home by lowly Bolton Wanderers in the FA Cup. It was a situation that did not go down well with many of the fans and the call for Souness's resignation was soon being openly mooted on the terraces. At the end of the season it did indeed seem that Souness was to be sacked but in an astonishing turn-around, he was given a vote of confidence by the board and further time to prove himself. But results never really improved and in January 1994, after Liverpool had been knocked out of the FA Cup by Bristol City, he was sacked. After some time in the wilderness and a libel case which brought him £500,000 in damages he was appointed manager of Galatasary, the Turkish club. Ironically the first three players he signed for his new club were three players he had sold at Liverpool.

SOUTH AFRICA. Liverpool have boasted a number of South African players over the years, including Jimmy Gray, Dirk Kemp, Arthur Riley, Gordon Hodgson, Bob Priday, Leslie Carr, Berry Nieuwenhuys, Doug Rudham, Craig Johnston and Bruce Grobbelaar. Four of them – Kemp, Rudham, Riley and Grobbelaar – were goalkeepers.

SPACKMAN, NIGEL. When manager Kenny Dalglish signed midfielder Nigel Spackman from Chelsea early in 1987 for £400,000, he looked a particularly impressive buy, but injury and loss of form were to dog his Anfield career. Perhaps Spackman never really had the consistency and two years later, after just 39 league appearances, he moved on to Queens Park Rangers, proving that even Kenny Dalglish could make mistakes in the transfer market. He later joined Glasgow Rangers.

SPEEDIE, DAVID. Signed from Coventry by Dalglish late in the 1990–91 season for £750,000, Speedie was an immediate success, scoring on his debut against Manchester United and then against Everton. Speedie had long been a target for the Liverpool crowd, yet the Kop soon forgave him once he was wearing a Liverpool shirt. But his career at Liverpool did not last long as his initial promise soon wore off. He was already past 30 when he joined the club and despite his early impact he could not settle into a role at Anfield. In many ways his signing smacked of panic. What Liverpool needed most were youngsters and someone who was English, rather than a 31-year-old Scot. New manager Graeme Souness had other plans for Speedie and in 1992 he was transferred to Blackburn Rovers, where ironically he was to link up eventually with the man who had brought him to Anfield, Kenny Dalglish. He had a highly successful stint at Ewood Park, scoring regularly in second division football, and helped push Blackburn into the Premier League. But once in the premier division Dalglish quickly let him go. Speedie was an aggressive terrier of a player, often getting into trouble. He had probably seen his best days at Chelsea. Born in Scotland, he had also played with Barnsley and Darlington. He was capped ten times by Scotland though never while as a Liverpool player.

SPICER, EDDIE. Liverpool-born Eddie Spicer began his Anfield career just before the Second World War but had to wait until 1946 before making his league debut. A full-back, Spicer was as courageous on the field as he had been during his army career when he was decorated for bravery. He won a league championship medal in his first season, 1946–47, and was a member of Liverpool's Cup final losing side in 1950. Spicer could play on either side of the defence, though he always claimed that he preferred being at left-back. During Liverpool's close season tour of Sweden in 1951 he broke a leg and missed the following season entirely. He did eventually return but towards the end of 1953 broke his leg again playing against Manchester United. He never played again.

SPONSORS. Liverpool were the first club in the Football League to announce a sponsorship deal when Hitachi became their official sponsors in 1979. A few years later Crown Paints took over and then Candy. Liverpool's current sponsors are Carlsberg, who pay £1 million a year for the privilege, with a four-year contract that stretches into 1996.

ST JOHN, IAN. Ian St John was the first Liverpool superstar of the modern era. He was signed from Motherwell in May 1961 for what was then a huge fee – £37,500 – and a record deal for Liverpool Football Club. But it was money well spent as St John lined up alongside Roger Hunt to form a striking partnership that was to set the seal for Liverpool's future. Although he was only a shade over 5ft 7ins, St John could outjump most defenders and had a power that belied his size and weight. He was strong, quick on the ball and showed neat control under pressure. The Kop loved him, especially his name: 'St John' became almost the first ever football chant and set a trend that continues on terraces to this day. At Motherwell he had already shown prowess in front of goal, scoring a notable hat trick in two and a half minutes – the fastest ever in Scottish football. And the style continued at Anfield where he adapted easily to the rigours of league soccer. He stepped straight into the Liverpool line-up and by the end of his first season had scored 18 league goals to add to the 41 scored by Roger Hunt. Liverpool were champions of the second division and even life in the first division did not deter their goalscoring partnership. The goals flowed for a couple of seasons but then began to dry up slowly as injury disrupted his appearances and he took on a new role in midfield. He scored the winning goal in the 1965 FA Cup final and collected a couple of league championship medals. After more than 400 appearances in the famous number nine shirt he quit Anfield to join Coventry City as assistant manager. He later played with Tranmere Rovers before returning to management with Motherwell and Portsmouth. He also had a stint as a coach at Sheffield Wednesday. Eventually he found his way into television and soon became part of another famous footballing duo – *The Saint and Greavsie Show*. In all he played 419 games for Liverpool, scoring 118 goals, and was capped 21 times by Scotland.

STAUNTON, STEVE. Blond-haired Irish full-back who made the break into the Liverpool first team during the 1988–89 season as injuries forced manager Dalglish to dig deep into his reserves. Staunton joined Liverpool from Dundalk in 1986 and soon began to collect Irish international honours. With the departure of Dalglish, however, he was sold to Aston Villa for £1.1 million. As a youth Staunton had also played Gaelic football and was the youngest ever player to win a senior championship medal. A quick defender, he was fond of chasing up the flanks, although his final ball into the area did not always match his runs. He made 65 league appearances for Liverpool.

STENSGAARD, MICHAEL. Roy Evans' first signing. Born in Denmark in September 1974, goalkeeper Michael Stensgaard was signed from Danish club Havidovre in 1994 for £300,000. Has yet to make his debut for Liverpool although he has sat on the substitutes' bench more times than he cares to remember and did play in a couple of pre-season friendlies. Injured for most of the 1994–95 season.

STEVENSON, WILLIE. Elegant left-half of the Shankly era. Willie Stevenson might well have been lost to English and Scottish football had Bill Shankly not rescued him from a life Down Under. After a dispiriting time at Glasgow Rangers, where he languished in the reserves following the signing of Jim Baxter, Stevenson decided to try his luck in Australia. But Shankly swooped quickly to pick up a bargain and over the next six seasons Stevenson played 237 games for the Reds, scoring 17 goals. 'Tall, sure and cultured' was how one football writer described him. Stevenson liked nothing more than to stride out, carrying the ball upfield. He was one of the early breed of creative midfielders and although he may not have scored as many goals as the Kop would have wished, his raids into foreign territory engineered many a goal. He won a Cup winners' medal in 1965 and a couple of league championship medals to add to the Cup and championship medals he had already claimed with Rangers. Stevenson eventually lost his place to Emlyn Hughes and in December 1967 he moved to Stoke City. He later had a season with Tranmere Rovers.

STEWART, PAUL. Manchester-born Paul Stewart began his

footballing days with Blackpool where he played more than 200 games. But it was at his next club, Manchester City, where he really began to excel, making 51 appearances and scoring an impressive 26 goals. It was more than enough to attract Tottenham, who in the face of enormous competition enticed him to White Hart Lane. Unfortunately he seemed to leave his shooting boots back in Lancashire and was never as prolific with the London club as he had been with City. Eventually he was converted into a midfielder, a move which seemed to spark off a revival in his career and brought him an FA Cup winners' medal in 1991. A year later Graeme Souness, in search of some much-needed strength in his midfield, was persuaded that Stewart was the man for the job and paid out £2.5 million to acquire his services. Yet despite his huge fee Stewart has failed to impress and much of his time at Anfield has been spent either in the reserves or out on loan.

STOLEN. Liverpool might have stolen a few games in their time but only once have they literally had a cup stolen from them. And ironically it was the first cup they ever lifted, the Lancashire League championship, which had been won in their first ever season, 1892–93. The cup was on display along with the Liverpool District Cup in a pawnbroker's shop when it was stolen on 1 September 1893. It was never recovered.

STORER, HARRY. Turn of the century goalkeeper. Storer joined Liverpool from Woolwich Arsenal in 1894. He made 121 appearances over the next five seasons but found himself out of favour at the beginning of the 1900–1 season and subsequently missed out on winning a league championship medal to add to his second division champions' medal. Storer was also a cricketer, playing six games for Derbyshire during the 1895 season.

STRONG, GEOFF. Another outstanding Shankly signing. Strong had already played more than a hundred games for

Arsenal when Shankly snapped him up in November 1964 for £40,000. It was hardly a sensational signing but Strong was to prove an inspiration. His strength was that he could play almost anywhere and he could also score goals. He had the knack of lying in wait for loose balls just outside the area and he struck many a crucial goal for Liverpool. Few were more important than his header against Celtic in the European Cup Winners' Cup semi-final at Anfield. Strong played in the 1965 Cup final and the following year won a league championship medal. In August 1970, after almost 200 games and 32 goals for Liverpool, he was sold to Coventry for £30,000.

STUBBINS, ALBERT. Wallsend boy Albert Stubbins was without doubt one of the heroes of Liverpool's post-war championship-winning side. Stubbins began his career in 1937 on Tyneside with Newcastle United and played with them throughout the war, scoring a total of 237 goals in 218 appearances. It was a remarkable record even though many of the games played during that period were of little consequence. When football resumed after the war Newcastle's fans expected much from him but just as the season opened he demanded a transfer. He was chased by numerous clubs but the race was finally between Liverpool and Everton. And it was Liverpool who eventually won though it cost them a record fee of £12,500. It was the first time Liverpool had ever paid out a five-figure fee for a player. But with Stubbins notching up 24 league goals in 36 outings in his first season it was money well spent. Stubbins, with his size 11 boots, was a natural goalscorer, a player of considerable skill as well as pace. After a couple of seasons, however, he asked for a move back to Tyneside. His family had never really settled on Merseyside but the Liverpool board refused his request. There followed a difficult period, with Stubbins refusing to re-sign. His goalscoring instinct went into cold storage. When eventually he relented, injury struck and his prowess as a goalscorer was never the same. He scored 24 league goals in each of his first two seasons at

Anfield but after that hit double figures only once over the next six years. His final goal tally for Liverpool was 83 goals in 180 games. He retired in 1954 and was on the scouting staff for a while. He also had a spell as national coach of the USA side, rekindling his youth which had been spent in the United States. In later life he was to be more widely remembered as a journalist back in his beloved north-east.

SUBSTITUTES. The first ever Liverpool substitute was Geoff Strong, who came on for Chris Lawler against West Ham United at Anfield on 15 September 1965, and scored an equaliser.

SUPER CUP. Liverpool have played in the European Super Cup on three occasions, winning it once.
1977 1st leg Hamburg 1 Liverpool 1
     2nd leg Liverpool 6 Hamburg 0 (Liverpool win 7–1 on aggregate)
1978 1st leg Anderlecht 3 Liverpool 1
     2nd leg Liverpool 2 Anderlecht 1 (Anderlecht win 4–3 on aggregate)
1985 Juventus 2 Liverpool 0

SUPER SUB. Nickname given to David Fairclough who made a habit of coming on as a substitute and scoring vital goals.

SUSPENSION. Liverpool's Kevin Keegan has the dubious honour of being the first ever English player to be sent off at Wembley when he and Billy Bremner were given their marching orders during the 1974 Charity Shield game between Liverpool and Leeds. Both players were suspended for six weeks, one of the longest ever suspensions given by the Football Association.

T

TALLEST PLAYER. It is impossible to say for definite who has been the tallest player ever on Liverpool's books as such records are notoriously unreliable. But almost certain to lay claim to the distinction is former goalkeeper Steve Ogrizovic who stood at 6ft 5in in his stockings. Of the outfield players Mark Wright at 6ft 3in must rank among the tallest, with South African Hugh Gerhadi, a 1950s inside-forward, topping even him at 6ft 4in.

TANNER, NICKY. If ever a player was to wake up and discover that a dream had come true it was Nicky Tanner. A midfielder with Bristol Rovers, Tanner arrived at his club one morning to be told that the chairman and secretary wished to speak with him. He had been having talks with bottom of the fourth division Torquay and was expected to join them on a free transfer. Instead when he arrived in the boardroom it was the Liverpool management who faced him. A nominal fee was agreed and Liverpool had little trouble in persuading Tanner to change his mind about going to Torquay. He had played just over 100 games for Rovers. His immediate chances at Anfield were to be limited and he did not break into the first team until

Graeme Souness arrived and injuries demanded his presence. But once he made the break into the first team, he did not disgrace himself. Unfortunately a serious back injury forced Tanner into early retirement but at least he had enjoyed a few moments of glory with more than 30 appearances during the 1991–92 season

TAYLOR, PHIL. Liverpool manager and player. Taylor was born in Bristol and began his playing career with Bristol Rovers in 1932. Four years later Liverpool paid £5,000 for his services and he began a long and illustrious career with the Reds that would stretch over the next 20 years. He made his debut for Liverpool in March 1936, soon converting from inside-right to right-half, but like so many pre-war footballers the arrival of war was to interrupt a blossoming career. He duly returned to league football when hostilities ceased but by then he was almost 30. He captained the Liverpool side that swept to the league title in 1947 and was also skipper of the 1950 Cup final side. In 1947 he was also capped three times by England. He continued playing until 1954, then 35 years old, but as Liverpool were relegated he decided to call it a day and took up a post on the coaching staff. He rose through the ranks to chief coach and when Don Welsh was taken ill he took over briefly as caretaker manager. When Welsh finally decided in 1956 that he could carry on no longer, it was inevitable that Taylor would succeed him. Liverpool were in the second division and over the next three years Taylor would experience the frustration of near misses as Liverpool repeatedly failed to gain promotion by a whisker. He even plunged into the transfer market, recruiting Scottish international goalkeeper Tommy Younger from Hibs and Johnny Wheeler from Bolton while local boy Alan A'Court won England honours. And of course there was an ageing Billy Liddell. There was potential but never quite enough to escape the lower league. Most of the players were living on past glory. By November 1959 Taylor was worn out; he could contribute no more and sensibly resigned.

TELEGRAPHIC. Liverpool's telegraphic address used to be 'goalkeeper', an appropriate enough address given the many outstanding goalkeepers the club has had on its books.

TELEVISION. Anfield was chosen by BBC Television as the venue for the first ever *Match of the Day* programme on 22 August 1964. The game was shown that evening on BBC 2 with a national audience of 75,000, not that many more than the 47,000 who watched inside Anfield. A black cat appeared on the pitch that day and chased around the Kop goal before disappearing into the crowd. It was to prove a lucky omen, not only for Liverpool but for the BBC's new programme which 30 years later was still going strong. Fittingly, Anfield was also the venue for the first ever colour transmission of a game on *Match of the Day* when Liverpool entertained West Ham on 15 November 1969. There was another television innovation in 1967 when four large television screens were erected at Anfield so that more spectators could watch the fifth round FA cup clash at Goodison between Everton and Liverpool, so staggering had been the demand for tickets: 64,000 were squeezed into Goodison while a further 40,000 watched the giant screens half a mile away at Anfield, giving a total of 104,000 watching, one of the highest attendances for any soccer match ever played in England.

TENNIS. During the 1920s and 1930s Anfield was the venue for a number of sports, tennis included. At the time the game was ruled by amateurs but professional tennis was beginning to emerge as money tempted many stars to turn professional. The game was played on boards laid out on the Anfield pitch and among those who appeared were the American champion Bill Tilden and the former Wimbledon champion Fred Perry.

TEST MATCHES. During the latter years of the 19th century promotion and relegation battles were settled by a series of play-offs, known as Test Matches. In their first season in the Football League, 1892–93, Liverpool, who had topped the second division, were forced to play Newton Heath, bottom of the first division. Liverpool won 2–0 and were duly promoted. The following year they were again involved in a Test Match. This time it was Liverpool who were the bottom club and Bury who were top of the second division. Bury won 1–0 and Liverpool were duly relegated. But a year later they were back in the Test Matches, this time as second division champions, playing the two bottom clubs from the first division, Small Heath and West Bromwich Albion. The games were played over two legs with Liverpool winning through to the first division.

TESTIMONIALS. Although the club has given testimonials to many players in its history, perhaps the most successful have been for Roger Hunt and Tommy Smith. Hunt's testimonial attracted a crowd of over 50,000, while Smith's, played against an England XI just days after he had helped Liverpool win their first European Cup, drew an even more impressive crowd. More than 54,000 turned up for the game at Anfield, with thousands locked out.

THOMAS, MICHAEL. Liverpool fans will always remember Michael Thomas for his injury-time goal at Anfield as Arsenal stole the Double from under Liverpool's noses in May 1989. Yet despite Thomas's appalling audacity the fans soon took to him when he joined Liverpool and in the 1992 Cup final he partly repaid his debt with a splendid volley that put the Reds on their way to another Cup final victory. Thomas began his footballing days with the Gunners, enjoying more than 200 games before sensationally switching to Liverpool in 1991 in a £1.5 million deal. Strong and aggressive, Thomas is at his best chasing the ball into the area and has already netted a useful tally of goals, including the first goal against Sunderland in the 1992 FA Cup final. Unfortunately he missed virtually the entire 1993–94 season through injury but returned briefly the following

Peter Thompson

season. As yet he has not really fulfilled the £1.5 million Liverpool paid for him.

THOMPSON, PETER. During the 1960s there were few more exciting sights in the Football League than to see Peter Thompson running at defenders, the ball at his feet, as red shirts swarmed towards the Kop. Thompson was a delight to watch – fast, exhilarating and with the trickery to mesmerise defenders. Shankly bought him for £35,000

207

from Preston North End. He was 21 and was already receiving rave notices. He made his Anfield debut in August 1963 and during the next nine seasons played just over 400 games, scoring 54 goals. In his first season at Anfield he won four England Under-23 caps and also played his first full international. He was eventually capped 16 times by England while at Anfield, collecting league and FA Cup honours as well. He played virtually all his games on the left-wing. He left Liverpool for Bolton Wanderers in January 1974, having long since handed over his number 11 shirt to Steve Heighway.

THOMPSON, PHIL. Tall, gangly and awkward, Thompson never looked the part of a rugged defender, yet he was to prove one of the sturdiest defenders in the English game throughout the 1970s. Born in Liverpool, he had supported the club from the Kop as a boy. He joined the staff straight from school, making his first appearance as an 18-year-old, and went on to captain the side in many triumphs. He became a regular during the 1973–74 season and remained there, injuries allowing, until 1983 when the emergence of Mark Lawrenson and Alan Hansen began to limit his opportunities. Few attackers ever got the better of Thompson, whose timing and determination made up for his frail looks. He won his first England cap in 1976 at the age of 22 and went on to play 42 internationals. He even skippered England on one occasion. One of the most honoured players in the game, Thompson ended his career with two European Cup medals, a UEFA medal, five league championships, an FA Cup medal and two League Cup medals. After a brief loan period with Sheffield United he joined the Bramall Lane side on a permanent basis in March 1985 but returned to Anfield to join the coaching staff in July 1986. He remained until the summer of 1992 when he was surprisingly sacked by new manager Graeme Souness, the man who had taken over the captaincy from him ten years previously. In all he played more than 450 games for Liverpool.

TOKYO. Liverpool have twice played in the Japanese capital, for the World Club championship. In 1981 they were defeated 3–0 by Flamengo of Brazil in front of 62,000 spectators. Three years later, they again lost, this time to Independiente of Argentina, watched by another full house of 62,000 at the Olympic Stadium.

TOSHACK, JOHN. The giant Welsh striker will always be remembered for his exciting goalscoring partnership with Kevin Keegan that carried Liverpool to European glory during the 1970s. Toshack was a near-record signing when he moved from Cardiff City to Anfield for a £110,000 in November 1970. Tall, dangerous and a supreme header of the ball, he went on to score almost a century of goals for Liverpool in eight seasons. Yet those statistics tell only half the tale. Toshack's ability was also in flicking balls down to Keegan, who would be instinctively lurking alongside him somewhere in the penalty area ready to scoop up the chances. During their period together Toshack carried off two UEFA Cup winners' medals, three league champion-ships and the FA Cup. Sadly he was forced to watch Liverpool's first European Cup victory from the subs' bench. A few months later his partner Keegan was gone and Kenny Dalglish had arrived. They might have worked together but Paisley preferred others. Recurring injuries were also limiting Toshack's appearances, as indeed they had throughout his Anfield days. The writing was clearly on the wall and in February 1978, with only a handful of games to his credit that season, he moved to fourth division Swansea City as player-manager. It was an inspired move. Four seasons later he was back at Anfield, having taken Swansea from the fourth to the top of the first division in consecutive seasons. But the dream did not last and with Swansea relegated Toshack took over the Portuguese side Sporting Lisbon, where he proved yet again that he had the magic touch. He later managed Real Sociedad and Real Madrid. Already a Welsh international before he arrived on Merseyside, Toshack added a further 26 caps to his name during his time at Anfield. A great favourite with the Kop, his name has been regularly mooted as a possible Liverpool manager although with time this looks to be increasingly unlikely. He was briefly manager of the Welsh national side but resigned after just one game in charge.

John Toshack

TOURS. For many years Liverpool avoided pre-season tours. One of their few pre-war trips was during the mid-1930s when they played a number of games in Prague. Their first ever tour was in 1906 when they visited France. After the war they became a little more adventurous and in 1947 toured the United States, but it was not until the club had tasted European football that they realised the importance of pre-season games as a useful means, not only of acclimatising themselves to continental football, but also of sorting out tactical and fitness problems before the domestic league season began in earnest.

TRANSFERS, RECORD. Liverpool have broken the British transfer record on a number of occasions, the most spectacular being the £440,000 paid to Glasgow Celtic for Kenny Dalglish. The £1.8 million for Peter Beardsley of Newcastle United was also a record deal between British clubs. And in June 1987 Liverpool received £3.2 million for striker Ian Rush, a record fee received by any British club. Dean Saunders was another record buy when he joined Liverpool from Derby County for £2.9 million in June 1991. Exactly four years later Liverpool again smashed the transfer record by paying out £8.5 million for the Nottingham Forest striker Stan Collymore.

TWENTYMAN, GEOFF. Perhaps won greater acclaim as Liverpool's chief scout than as a player. He came to Anfield from Carlisle United in December 1953 for £10,000 as a centre-half, but with Laurie Hughes still coveting the number five shirt Twentyman reverted to left-half. In all, he played 170 games for the Reds, scoring 18 goals before joining Ballymena United as player-manager in March 1959. He later had a further spell with Carlisle before returning to Anfield as chief scout in 1967. As Shankly's eyes up and down the country, Twentyman was responsible for bringing many fine youngsters from the lower divisions to Anfield, including Ray Clemence, Brian Hall and Steve Heighway. In his time he probably cast an eye over virtually every player Liverpool signed during the next 20 years. In the summer of 1987 he was surprisingly sacked by Liverpool and replaced by Ron Yeats, but he was immediately hired again by Graeme Souness at Glasgow Rangers. Virtually his last recommendations to Liverpool had been to buy John Barnes and Peter Beardsley.

U

UEFA CUP. Formerly known as the Fairs Cup, its name was changed in 1971 when it became the UEFA Cup. Liverpool first participated in the Fairs Cup in 1967. Although they reached a semi-final in 1971 they had little luck in the competition until its name changed. In their first season in the UEFA Cup, 1972–73, Liverpool went on to lift the trophy, beating Borussia Moenchengladbach in the two-legged final. Three years later they were once more successful, this time beating Bruges in the final. Liverpool did not compete in the competition again until the 1991–92 season when they reached the quarter-final before being beaten by Genoa. It was their first defeat in 16 rounds.

UNDEFEATED. In their first season in league soccer, 1893–94, Liverpool went an entire season without defeat to win the second division championship. They played 28 games, winning 22 and drawing six. They won all 14 of their home games.

UNDEFEATED – AT HOME. Between January 1978 and January 1981 Liverpool went 85 home games without defeat. The total was made up of 63 league games, nine

League Cup games, seven European games and six FA Cup games. This is a Football League record.

UNDEFEATED – FROM START OF SEASON. From the start of the 1987–88 season Liverpool went 29 games before they were finally beaten, eventually losing to Everton. This equalled the record of Leeds United although, as all Liverpool fans know, Liverpool won more games during their run than Leeds.

UNDERWOOD, DAVID. During the early to mid-1950s Liverpool went through an unusual spell in that they could never settle on a permanent goalkeeper. After Cyril Sidlow had left the club, a number of goalkeepers were tried but all with only limited success. One of these was Dave Under-wood, a tall, athletic Cockney. Underwood joined the club from Watford for £7,000 in December 1953 and went straight into the first team. But Liverpool were already in deep trouble and Underwood could not help them stave off relegation. The following season he lost his place and although he returned briefly the season after that, his days at Anfield were clearly numbered. In July 1956 he returned to Watford for the knockdown fee of £1,250. He made just 45 league appearances.

UNIVERSITY. Liverpool have had a number of university graduates over the years. The first was almost certainly Gerald Powys Dewhurst, who played just one game at centre-forward for the club in 1894. Dewhurst was a graduate of Cambridge University and had won a Blue in 1892–94. A fine amateur, he also played for the Corinthians between 1892 and 1895 and appeared for England against Wales in 1895. Arthur Berry was another graduate, this time from Oxford, who made four appearances for Liverpool in 1908. He was also the holder of two soccer gold medals from the 1908 and 1912 Olympics. During the 1920s the Reverend James Jackson attended Liverpool University where he was studying for the ministry while still playing for Liverpool. He later attended Cambridge University. In more recent years other graduates have included Steve Heighway, a graduate of Warwick University, and Brian Hall, a graduate of Manchester University, as well as goalkeeper Mike Hooper.

UREN, HAROLD. The Bristol-born Harold Uren joined Liverpool as an amateur from Hoylake in 1907, turning professional two years later. He was a tricky little winger who played 43 games for the club after making his debut in November 1907. Four years later Everton stepped in and signed him in exchange for the Irish international Bill Lacey and Tom Gracie. Liverpool clearly got the better of the deal as Uren played just 24 games for Everton, while Lacey and Gracie went on to play 250 games between them for the Reds. Uren eventually wound up at Wrexham.

USA. Immediately after winning the league championship in 1948 Liverpool embarked on a summer tour of the United States. It was the first time they had ever ventured to America and it proved to be beneficial in more than one way. Perhaps the most successful aspect of the tour was the eventual signing from Brooklyn Wanderers of centre-half Joe Cadden. Liverpool had played Brooklyn in a friendly and were immediately impressed by Cadden, who soon became the first player to be signed from an American club. Cadden had been born in Glasgow but after the war made his way to the United States. He played just four games for Liverpool before he was transferred to Grimsby.

Barry Venison

V

VENISON, BARRY. Was one of the youngest ever Sunderland captains when he skippered them to the League Cup final in 1985 and certainly the youngest ever player to lead a team out at Wembley. He was just 20 years old. A year later he joined Liverpool, the only club to bother taking up his round robin letter to first division clubs offering his services. At £250,000 he was worth a try and soon turned into a bargain buy. An effective, uncomplicated, full-back who liked to work his way forward, he had a vicious shot and struck a number of goals from the edge of the penalty area. He made well over 100 appearances for Liverpool and would have had many more but for injury. He won a league championship medal and a Cup-winners' medal with the club before Graeme Souness sold him to Newcastle during the summer of 1992 for £250,000. Venison has been capped at full England and Under-21 level, and played 158 games for Liverpool.

VICTORIES IN A SEASON – HIGHEST. In the 1978–79 season Liverpool won 30 of their 42 league fixtures to win the league title, the highest in the club's history.

VICTORIES IN A SEASON – LOWEST. Liverpool's poorest performance was in 1894–95 when they won only seven matches out of their 30 league games and finished bottom of the first division. In modern times their worst record was 1953–54 when they managed only nine wins out of the 42 games and were duly relegated.

VICTORY INTERNATIONALS. Liverpool had a number of players represent their country during the Victory and wartime internationals. The most notable were Billy Liddell, who made eight appearances for Scotland, and Matt Busby, who played seven times for Scotland. Ray Lambert made seven appearances for Wales.

VIDEOS. Liverpool have produced a number of videos in conjunction with the BBC, the most notable being an official history of the club.

WADDLE, ALAN. Although centre-forward Alan Waddle made just a handful of appearances for the club during the 1970s, he is fondly remembered as a player who always stood on the brink of a breakthrough into first team football. But with John Toshack and Kevin Keegan around his chances were always going to be limited. He came to Liverpool from Halifax Town in June 1973 and left four years later to join Leicester City. After that he played with a host of clubs, including Newport, Peterborough, Swansea and Mansfield, making a total of 289 league outings and scoring 76 goals. Just 16 of those appearances were with Liverpool.

WADSWORTH, HAROLD. The former Tranmere Rovers winger Harold Wadsworth was also the younger brother of Liverpool centre-half Walter Wadsworth. Born in Bootle in 1898, Harold Wadsworth joined Liverpool in 1918 and went on to make 54 league appearances. In 1924 he moved on to Leicester where he helped them to the second division championship and later had stints at Nottingham Forest and Millwall.

WADSWORTH, WALTER. Walter Wadsworth enjoyed a far more successful career with Liverpool than his younger brother Harold. He came to Anfield shortly before the First World War, making his league debut in March 1915. Built more like a slim-line modern centre-half rather than the traditional hefty version, Wadsworth soon became a vital component in the Liverpool side that went on to win two league championships during the early 1920s. Yet surprisingly he was never capped by his country. He was always keen to sneak upfield and in a career that took in 240 games he even managed eight goals. In May 1926 he joined Bristol City and subsequently played with New Brighton. He was commonly known as 'Big Waddy'.

WALKER, JOHN. Inside-right of the Victorian era who came to Liverpool from Heart of Midlothian in 1898. He stayed for just four seasons, making 133 appearances and scoring 31 goals. Walker was already a well-honoured player when he arrived at Anfield, having collected league championship and Scottish Cup medals with Hearts, as well as three Scottish international caps. At Liverpool he added another league championship medal to his growing collection. And it was Walker's goal in the final game that clinched the title for Liverpool in 1901. In 1902 he returned north, joining Glasgow Rangers where he enjoyed a third outstanding career, winning two more Scottish caps and a Scottish Cup winners' medal.

WALL, PETER. Left-back who never quite made the grade despite much promise. Signed from Wrexham in October 1966, Wall always seemed to be on the verge of a breakthrough but usually he was simply filling in for an injured colleague and never succeeded in taking over. He made 31 league appearances before joining Crystal Palace in May 1970 for £35,000 where he enjoyed far more success.

WALLACE, GORDON. Scottish inside-left who joined

Liverpool as an apprentice but failed to make the break-through as a regular first team player. He made just 19 appearances in the league for Liverpool before joining Crewe Alexandra in October 1967.

WALSH, JAMES. Stockport-born centre-forward of the 1920s who arrived at Anfield in June 1922 from his local club Stockport County. He turned out to be a useful buy, equally happy anywhere up front, and went on to play 68 league games for Liverpool, scoring 24 goals. In 1925 he toured Australia with the Football Association, playing three times against Australia. He joined Hull City during the summer of 1928 and later played with Crewe and Colwyn Bay.

WALSH, PAUL. Young attacker signed from Luton Town in May 1984 for a club record fee of £700,000. Already an England international with three caps to his credit, much was expected of Walsh whose ball control had excited fans throughout the country. Walsh, though, never really settled at Anfield and certainly never fulfilled the potential that his skills had promised. Injury cost him his place just as he was beginning to forge a useful partnership with Rush and Dalglish and he never really established himself again as a regular first team player. Incidents outside of football also affected his Anfield career. He seemed to lack the necessary discipline and commitment and Walsh eventually went the same way as so many potentially talented players. In February 1988 Liverpool were only too happy to let him return south where he joined Tottenham Hotspur for £500,000. His career at Spurs followed similar lines – a bruising row with Ray Clemence, the occasional delightful display but little overall consistency. In 63 league games at Anfield he scored 25 goals.

WALTERS, MARK. One of Graeme Souness's first signings when he took over as manager. Souness had originally signed the young winger when he was manager at Glasgow

Rangers, paying Aston Villa £600,000. When he signed him again in August 1991 he cost Liverpool £1.25 million. In his early years Walters had looked an exciting prospect, gaining England youth and Under-21 international honours. At Rangers he had attracted glowing reports, with his snaky runs down the flanks even earning him an England cap. But the return to English league football proved to be more difficult. Injury kept him out of the side for some time and when he did appear he often looked lightweight and easily shaken off the ball. He did occasionally bring a dash of excitement to the side and probably no more so than with his two goals against Blackburn Rovers at Anfield in December 1992. He was a member of the 1992 FA Cup-winning side. Since then his appearances have been limited, partly through injury as well as form. At one point he was loaned out to Wolves and appeared to be on the verge of leaving Anfield.

WAR. Liverpool have lost a number of players fighting for their country. During the First World War Joe Dines, a soccer gold medallist in the 1912 Olympics, was killed in action on the Western Front. The winger Wilfred Bartrop also lost his life towards the end of the Great War while serving as a gunner in the Royal Field Artillery. He made just three appearances for Liverpool but had been a member of Barnsley's Cup-winning side of 1912. Tom Gracie died in 1915, aged 26, while serving as a corporal in the Royal Scots Guard. Frank Grayer, a right-back who made just one appearance for Liverpool in 1914, was badly wounded at Ypres during the First World War and never played football again. During the Second World War Tom Cooper, the England full-back, was killed following a motor-cycle accident while serving with the military police.

WAR DECORATIONS. A number of Liverpool players were decorated for bravery during the Second World War. They included Berry Nieuwenhuys, who served with the

RAF and was awarded the Czech Medal of Merit, and Bill Jones, who was awarded the Military Medal for rescuing wounded comrades while under fire. During the First World War half-back George Lathom was awarded the Military Cross when he served as a captain with the Royal Welsh Fusiliers.

WAR FOOTBALL. Liverpool, like most clubs, continued to play football during both world wars even though the normal Football League programme had been suspended. During the First World War they played in the Lancashire section of the league and were extremely successful. In the Second World War they again played in a regional league, this time the Football League North. There was also a guesting system which allowed players from other clubs to play for a side close to where they were barracked.

WARK, JOHN. A surprise £450,000 signing from Ipswich Town in March 1984. Even though he was already 27 at the time, Wark proved to be an inspired buy by manager Joe Fagan in Liverpool's push for a third consecutive title. The following season he was even more devastating, scoring 18 league goals in 40 appearances, although it was not quite enough to give Liverpool a fourth consecutive league title. However, his five goals in European competition certainly edged Liverpool towards another European final and he ended the season with a total of 27 goals in all competitions. Midfielder Wark, who had enjoyed a long and successful career with Ipswich, was a good-value player, always committed, determined and consistent. He was a strong, aggressive runner who seemed to sense when space would open up in front of him and was always prepared to chase or run with the ball. He was also brave, ready to go in where the boots were flying. Unfortunately his talents were often overshadowed in a Liverpool side that included world-class players like Dalglish, Rush, Hansen, Lawrenson and Souness. Yet his contribution should never be underestimated. Born in Glasgow, he won his first Scotland cap in

John Wark

1979 and his 29th and final cap six years later. In 1981 he was also the PFA Player of the Year and at Anfield went on to add further medals to the UEFA Cup winners' medal he had already collected with Ipswich. However, a broken leg in 1986 effectively ended his Liverpool career and in January 1988 he returned to his old club Ipswich for £100,000. To the surprise of many he fought his way back to fitness and was soon displaying again his tough, talented style – a feature Liverpool could well have done with in subsequent years. He also had a short period with Middlesbrough but returned to Ipswich for a third spell in 1992, still looking as sprightly and aggressive as ever. He played a total of 64 league games for Liverpool, scoring 28 goals. Wark also holds a joint European record of having scored 14 goals in Europe in a single season.

WATKINSON, WILLIAM. Joined Liverpool in 1946 from Prescot Cables but managed only 24 league appearances and a couple of goals in the first division before moving on to Accrington Stanley in January 1951. He later played with Halifax Town. A right-winger, Watkinson never stood much chance when Liverpool already had an abundance of wingers on hand.

WATSON, ALEX. Just three appearances for Liverpool before he joined Derby County. Watson, the brother of the Everton and England defender Dave Watson, joined Liverpool straight from school in 1984. He made his league debut in March 1988 and although he always looked a promising prospect there was so much defensive talent at Anfield that it was never convenient to give him a long run in the first team. He did make one Wembley appearance with Liverpool, lining up against Wimbledon in the Charity Shield. He later played with Bournemouth.

WATSON, TOM. Tom Watson was one of the outstanding figures in the early history of football, the man largely responsible for putting Newcastle, Sunderland and Liverpool on the footballing map. Prior to joining Liverpool he was in charge at Sunderland where he created the great Sunderland side known as the 'team of all talents' that went on to win so many honours. In August 1896 John McKenna, then secretary at Liverpool, managed to persuade Watson south to Anfield to take over as secretary/manager. Watson was to prove an inspired choice as he guided Liverpool to two championships and laid the foundation for the club's future. It was Watson who brought players like Alec Raisbeck, Elisha Scott, Sam Hardy and Sam Raybould to Anfield. Under Watson

Liverpool won two league titles and a second division championship, and appeared in the FA Cup final. It was a remarkable achievement, adding to the many championships he had already brought Sunderland. Watson remained at the helm at Anfield until his death in May 1915.

WELFARE, HENRY. Made just four appearances on the wing for Liverpool immediately prior to the First World War. But his main claim to fame was that he emigrated to Brazil at the end of the 1913–14 season, initially joining the Corinthians Club but eventually signing for the Fluminense club. He helped them to win the Brazilian title three years in succession. Welfare soon became one of Brazil's best known players where he was commonly nicknamed 'Celso'. He spent the rest of his days in Brazil and died in Rio in 1961.

WELSH, DON. Liverpool manager for five years during the early 1950s. Unfortunately Welsh was at Anfield at a period which coincided with one of the club's lowest points. He arrived in 1951 from Charlton and was already well known to Liverpool fans, having guested for the club regularly during the war years. As a player with Charlton he had seen the London club rise from the depths of third division football to the top of the first division and two FA Cup finals in just a few seasons. As skipper of that side Welsh had been inspirational and it was hardly surprising that someone should offer him a job in management. One of those clubs was Liverpool and he arrived at Anfield in 1951 to find the club already in poor shape. The post-war championship-winning side had aged and what new talent that had been introduced had proved to be poor by comparison. It was Welsh who was forced to undertake the thankless task of rebuilding. Unfortunately the slide had already gone too far and the club's directors seemed reluctant to dig into their pockets to buy themselves out of trouble. The result was inevitable. They narrowly avoided relegation in 1953 but a year later could do nothing to avoid the drop. Life in the second division proved to be just as grim, with no quick return to the higher division. They were trounced 9–1 at Birmingham and then in the final game of the season crashed 6–1 at Rotherham. But at least those defeats forced the directors to cough up some money. Sadly, Welsh was not the smartest of operators in the transfer market, though the team did eventually end up narrowly missing promotion. But for the directors who had been assured that money would win them their place back in the first division it was not enough and Welsh duly became the first and only Liverpool manager to be sacked.

Don Welsh

WEMBLEY. Liverpool have made more appearances at Wembley than any other Football League club. Up to the beginning of the 1993–94 season they had played there on 30 occasions in major games, having made nine appearances in the FA Cup final, seven in the League Cup final, 13 in the

Charity Shield and one in a European Cup final. They have also taken part in a couple of minor competitive games at Wembley.

WEST, ALF. Pre-First World War defender who enjoyed two separate spells with Liverpool. He was a right-back, though he was equally at home on the left, who came to Liverpool from Barnsley in 1903 and was a member of the club's championship-winning side of 1906. He left Anfield in 1909, joining Reading, but returned a year later for a second spell, though that lasted only a season before he signed for Notts County. He made a total of 128 league appearances for Liverpool.

WHEELER, JOHN. Wheeler was one of the more success-ful players in a Liverpool side that struggled to escape the second division for much of the 1950s. He came to Anfield in 1956 via Tranmere Rovers and Bolton Wanderers and over the next seven years went on to make 177 appearances, scoring 23 goals. He was essentially a right-half with a hard tackle but liked to get forward and had a sharp eye for goal. For a while he was even the Liverpool captain but Wheeler had probably enjoyed his most successful days at Bolton where he had been a member of the 1953 FA Cup final side and had won an England cap. By the time he arrived at Anfield his best days were over, though he was still a useful servant to the club, playing on into his thirties. By the time Liverpool finally escaped the lower division his days were over and he made just one appearance during the second division championship season, 1961–62. The following season he was gone, eventually settling down as a coach at Bury. Wheeler also won England B honours and played for the Football League.

WHELAN, RONNIE. Left-sided midfielder. Intelligent, neat and accomplished and equally adept in attack as defence. Whelan was another outstanding Paisley signing when he came from Home Farm in Ireland for next to

Ronnie Whelan

nothing in October 1979. After spending the usual season in reserve football learning the Liverpool way, he graduated into the first team during the 1981–82 season although he had managed one league appearance, even scoring on his debut, the season before. From then on he was to be a regular, only forced out through injury. Slim and agile, Whelan's strength belied his appearance and he could be just as effective a ball winner as any midfielder. Above all he had fine distribution and, having won the ball, his accurate passing set up attacks with remarkable speed. He could even weave his own way into the area and scored many a vital goal for Liverpool, particularly during his first full season when his ten league goals in 31 games were paramount in bringing the championship to Anfield. It was to bring him the first of six championship medals. On top of that he went on to win a European Cup winners' medal, two FA Cup medals and three League Cup medals, making him one of the most honoured players in the game. Whelan won his first Irish cap at the age of 20 in 1981 and has gone on to collect more than 30 caps for his country. In 1994 he joined Southend United after more than 430 appearances for the club.

WHITE, DICK. Centre-half during the dark days of division two football. Signed from Scunthorpe in 1955, he went on to make more than 200 league appearances for the Reds before Ron Yeats arrived at Anfield to take over the number five shirt. As a result White was pushed deeper into defence and was a member of the side that lifted the second division championship in 1962. He played just 24 times that season. It was clear that his days were numbered and at the end of that season he was transferred to Doncaster Rovers for £4,000.

WHITHAM, JACK. Seven goals in 15 appearances just about sums up Jack Whitham's Anfield career. He was signed in April 1970 from Sheffield Wednesday where injury had dogged his career and although he was to be more lucky in that respect at Anfield he was to prove unlucky in facing some fierce competition for places upfront. Toshack, Boersma, Heighway, Waddle and later Keegan were all contenders for those roles. In the end he gave up and in 1974 moved to Cardiff City.

WILKINSON, BARRY. Member of the Liverpool side

relegated at the end of the 1953–54 season. He signed in 1953 from the famous amateur club Bishop Auckland, which had also spawned Bob Paisley. Half-back Wilkinson immediately slotted into the Liverpool line-up and went on to make 78 league appearances, but he was part of the Shankly clear-out in 1960 when he was transferred to Bangor City. Later he had a spell with Tranmere Rovers.

WILLIAMS, ROBERT BRIAN. Liverpool-born player who was happy to play almost anywhere. He made his league debut in March 1949 and made 31 league appearances over the next four seasons, scoring five goals. Most of his games were as an inside-forward and he was one of the first players to develop the long throw-in technique. He left Anfield in 1953, initially joining South Liverpool but later had a spell with Crewe Alexandra.

WILLIAMS, T. V. Liverpool chairman for many years and the man largely responsible for bringing Bill Shankly to Anfield. He is generally regarded as one of the finest chairmen in the club's history. Thomas Valentine Williams was a director of the club from 1947 until his death and was chairman between 1956 and 1964.

WILSON, CHARLIE. A loyal Liverpool servant who remained with the club as player, skipper and trainer for almost 40 years. He signed from Stockport in 1899 when he was the target of both Liverpool and Manchester City. Wilson initially wanted to sign for City but Liverpool offered him £100 out of the transfer money and so he was tempted to Anfield instead. Unfortunately the £100 was never forthcoming. It took Wilson a couple of seasons to establish himself but once he was settled Liverpool went on to clinch their first league championship in 1901. He was a sturdy little half-back, hard in the tackle and fast on his feet. A broken leg against Middlesbrough, however, robbed him and Liverpool of many more appearances. He managed just another 29 league outings over the next four seasons before he finally gave up playing. He was even officially a member of the side that clinched the league championship in 1906, although he never actually played a game that season. In the long run his premature retirement was to prove a blessing as he took on the job of scout and later trainer and coach, proving an outstanding success. He was to be coach of the side that clinched two league titles in the early 1920s and was a vital part of the club during so many of its early successes.

WINS. The club record for the number of league wins over a season is 30 during the 1978–79 season.

WORLD CLUB CHAMPIONSHIP. Liverpool have twice competed in the World Club championship after winning the European Cup. In 1977 and 1978 they decided not to compete but in 1981 they played Flamengo of Brazil in a one-off match in Japan and lost 3–0. In 1984 they again competed in a one-off game in Tokyo, this time against Independiente of Argentina, losing 1–0.

WRIGHT, DAVID. A 1930s centre-forward who slotted into a famous goalscoring line that included Gordon Hodgson and Sam English. Wright was never quite as prolific as the others but still managed 35 goals in 93 league appearances. The signing of English, however, forced Liverpool to play Wright at inside-left, a position he never really enjoyed, and after just a dozen games he quit the club, joining Hull City for £1,000. Born in Kirkcaldy, Wright began his football with Cowdenbeath before joining Sunderland where his career really began to blossom. In March 1930 he cost Liverpool a mammoth £8,000, although this did include another player. His career at Hull was surprisingly short and sparse of goals and a year later he was on his way to Bradford. He had just one more season in league football before retiring; he was still only 30. It had been a strange and sudden decline to what had been a successful goal-scoring career at Anfield.

WRIGHT, VIC. Took over from his namesake David Wright during the mid-1930s, doubling up as a centre-forward or inside-forward. Born in Walsall, Wright had done the rounds before arriving at Anfield, having played with Bristol City, Rotherham United twice and Sheffield Wednesday. He signed for Liverpool in March 1934 and went on to make 81 league appearances, scoring 31 goals. He was transferred to Plymouth in June 1937.

WRIGHT, MARK. One of Graeme Souness's first signings in a double deal that also brought Dean Saunders from Derby County to Anfield during the summer of 1991. A tall, strong, central defender who had excelled in an England shirt, Wright enjoyed a useful first season at Anfield. But after that a loss of confidence and injury found him relegated to the reserves where his future remained in some doubt. Wright's footballing career began with Oxford United in 1981 but after just ten games and still only 18 he was transferred to Southampton for £230,000. He was an immediate success and the following season Southampton finished runners-up in the league. Wright made his full England debut when only 20 and although his international career kicked off to a nervous start he has gone on to pick up more than 40 England caps. Injury kept him out of the 1986 World Cup finals but in 1990, after having been ignored for some time, he proved to be one of the most effective defenders in the entire tournament, even heading the only goal of the game against Egypt. He had joined Derby County for a club record fee of £760,000 in 1987.

X

X. In football X traditionally stands for a draw. The club record for the number of draws in a season was in 1951–52 when they managed 19 draws out of 42 matches.

XMAS DAY. There was a time when football was regularly played on Christmas Day but in recent years the footballing authorities have dropped the fixture from their calendar. The last time Liverpool played on a Christmas Day was in 1958 when they lost 3–1 at Grimsby in a second division match. The next day they beat the same team 3–2 at Anfield with Billy Liddell netting a couple. One of the most memorable Christmas Day games was in 1925 when Liverpool beat Newcastle United 6–3 at Anfield, with Harry Chambers scoring a hat trick. The following day they lost 3–0 in the return at St James Park.

Y

YEATS, RON. When Bill Shankly signed the giant centre-half from Dundee United in July 1961 he invited journalists to walk around him. 'He's a colossus,' he told them and promised that Yeats would take Liverpool back to their rightful spot at the top of the first division. Yeats was the key to Shankly's plans and over the next ten years he would continue to be the backbone of a Liverpool team that founded a new glorious era. The 6ft 2in Scot cost Liverpool a record £30,000 but proved to be worth every penny. He was an old-fashioned type of centre-half, relying on his strength and aerial ability to ward off attackers, and there were few better at the job in the entire Football League. He made a total of 450 appearances in a red shirt and even managed 15 goals, mostly with his head. Shankly immediately made him captain and in 1965 Yeats, or 'Rowdy' as the fans liked to call him, became the first Liverpool player to lift the FA Cup. In his first season he had helped steer Liverpool to the second division title and in 1964 picked up the first of his two league championship medals. In 1966 he also collected a European Cup Winners' Cup runners-up medal, but surprisingly he was only capped twice by his country, something which always angered Shankly. In

Ron Yeats

December 1971 he moved over the water to Tranmere Rovers as player-assistant manager, later becoming manager. But it was not a particularly successful venture and he was sacked in April 1975. He returned to Anfield in 1986 as chief scout.

YOUNGER, TOMMY. There was little to cheer in the Liverpool side of the late 1950s yet one player who always looked convincing was goalkeeper Tommy Younger. Tall, well-built and with a thatch of blond curly hair, Younger was a majestic heir to the tradition of Liverpool goal-keepers. He was safe, agile and consistent. Younger joined Liverpool from Hibernian in June 1956 for £9,000. By then he was already a Scottish international and had been a member of the Hibs side that had won two Scottish league titles. Unfortunately he added little else to his collection at Anfield other than 16 more well-deserved international caps. Surprisingly he stayed just three seasons, making 127 appearances before joining Falkirk as player-manager. He was still only 29. Eight months later he retired through injury but made a dramatic comeback with Stoke and then had a spell at Leeds United. He eventually quit in October 1962 to become a scout for Leeds. He finally wound up back in Scotland with his first love Hibernian, where he became public relations officer and also a director. There then followed a highly successful career as a football administrator and at the time of his unexpected death in January 1984 he was the President of the Scottish Football Association.

YOUNGEST PLAYER. The youngest player to ever pull on a Liverpool shirt is Phil Charnock, who at the age of 17 came on as a substitute for Liverpool against Apollon Limassol at Anfield on 16 September 1992.

Z

ZENITH. Fans will argue over which moment has been the finest in the club's history. Among the chief contenders must be the winning of the club's first European Cup in Rome in 1977 and the defeat of their great rivals Everton in the 1986 FA Cup final to clinch the league and Cup double.